Conversations with William H. Gass

Literary Conversations Series

Peggy Whitman Prenshaw
General Editor

Photo credit: © Joyce Ravid

Conversations
with William H. Gass

Edited by
Theodore G. Ammon

University Press of Mississippi
Jackson

Books by William H. Gass

Omensetter's Luck. New York: New American Library, 1966.
Willie Masters' Lonesome Wife. Evanston, Ill.: Northwestern University Press, 1968.
In the Heart of the Heart of the Country, and Other Stories. New York: Harper & Row, 1968.
Fiction and the Figures of Life. New York: Knopf, 1970.
On Being Blue: A Philosophical Inquiry. Boston: D. R. Godine, 1975.
The World Within the Word. New York: Knopf, 1978.
The Habitations of the Word: Essays. New York: Simon and Schuster, 1985.
The Tunnel. New York: Knopf: Distributed by Random House, 1995.
Finding a Form: Essays. New York: Knopf: Distributed by Random House, 1996.
Cartesian Sonata & Other Novellas. New York: Knopf, 1998.
Reading Rilke: Reflections on the Problems of Translation. New York: Knopf, 1999.
Tests of Time. New York: Knopf: Distributed by Random House, 2002.

www.upress.state.ms.us

The University Press of Mississippi is a member of the Association of American University Presses.

⊗

Library of Congress Cataloging-in-Publication Data

Gass, William H., 1924–
   Conversations with William H. Gass / edited by Theodore G. Ammon.
      p.   cm.—(Literary conversations series)
   Includes index.
   ISBN: 978-1-61703-701-6
   1. Gass, William H., 1924– —Interviews.   2. Novelists, American—20th
century—Interviews.   3. Fiction—Authorship.   I. Ammon, Theodore G., 1954–
II.   Title.   III.   Series.
PS3557.A845 Z463   2003
813'.54—dc21   2002038010

British Library Cataloging-in-Publication Data available

Contents

Introduction

William H. Gass studied philosophy under Max Black at Cornell, wrote his dissertation on metaphor, and taught philosophy at Purdue and then Washington University in St. Louis for decades until his recent retirement. Yet his considerable reputation is based almost entirely upon fiction and upon essays which are more akin to literary criticism than traditional philosophy. Although his essays are thoroughly embedded in philosophical traditions, Gass does not compose tight philosophical arguments and publish them in the appropriate philosophical journals.

Gass claims to G. M. A. Janssens in the *Dutch Quarterly Review,* "Oh Well, I am not a philosopher at all; I just teach philosophy. . . . Second-rate philosophers are dreary, really dreary beyond belief, and how many great philosophers are there?" Gass is a rarity: a philosopher who has never pretended to be a philosopher, nor even do philosophy. So, on the one hand, perhaps Gass is not a philosopher, at least not by the current standards of the profession, and thus not a second-rate philosopher at all. He is, however, one of the finest essayists, fiction writers, and literary critics in English.

On the other hand, it's difficult to reconcile Gass's presence in literary essays with the fact that he refused to study literature in academia. "I didn't take any courses in English while I was at Kenyon. . . . I found that I fought English classes. I was such a smartass I thought I knew much more than the instructor," Gass confesses to Thomas LeClair in the *Paris Review.* "I write slowly because I write badly. I have to rewrite everything many, many times just to achieve mediocrity."

This from a man who spends more time mastering the sentence and the paragraph than anyone since Gertrude Stein? Yet Gass's self-criticism is not an exaggerated false modesty, as he makes clear in an interview from Joe David Bellamy's edited anthology, *The New Fiction:* "I wrote terrible poetry in my youth. I write doggerel now. I am a rotten poet and have absolutely no talent for it. I haven't the dramatic imagination at all. Even my characters tend to turn away from one another and talk to the void" (McCauley). William Gass is an absolutely uncompromising writer who has always demanded of himself an almost impossible artistic integrity. He can't go on, but he does go on, and although his view of the world is not as bleak as Beckett's, he shares much of Beckett's absurdist aesthetic. For Gass, superb writing is not merely difficult, but a process that is, in the Wittgensteinian spirit, wrenching and that is accompanied with ulcerous anger, exasperated pacing, decades of rewrites, and ultimately a dismissal of the finished product as something that is a tomb for the author.

"I write because I hate. A lot. Hard," Gass says to LeClair. "I wish to make my hatred acceptable because my hatred is much of me, if not my best part" (*Paris Review*). Should we take seriously that this passage, from Gass's groundbreaking novel *Omensetter's Luck,* is born of hate? "Brackett Omensetter was a wide and happy man. He could whistle like the cardinal whistles in the deep snow, or whirr like the shy 'white rising from its cover, or be the lark a-chuckle at the sky. He knew the earth. He put his hands in water. He smelled the clean fir smell. He listened to the bees. And he laughed his deep loud, wide and happy laugh whenever he could—which was often, long, and joyfully."[1]

Anyone who meets, talks with, or interviews William Gass cannot square his comments with the gentle man of letters who answers questions put to him with patience, grace, and honesty, nor square this alleged disposition with the reveries at the core of his writing, even if he explicitly says that his writing is bitter and that he writes to get even (LeClair, *Paris Review*). Of course it is *possible* to imagine William H. Gass as a curmudgeonly and bitter old man, lashing out at the world through his fiction for the sins of his parents and out of disgust for the meanness of humanity in general, perhaps trying to dignify and justify his own obsessions through art. One could choose passages from his 1995 novel *The Tunnel* that are as cynical as the above passage from *Omensetter's Luck* is playful and innocent. William H. Gass is not an easy man to grasp; and, like the man, his work is beautiful, formidable, and troubling all at once.

The interviews in this volume span at least twenty-five years and, although Gass believes that in interviews writers are notoriously evasive to the point of lying about their own work, there is considerable consistency here, and scarcely a hint of evasion, unless one is prepared to say that Gass has been consistently lying for twenty-five years. Not likely. In an *Iowa Review* interview conducted with writer Stanley Elkin, Gass even expresses mild exasperation because Elkin refuses to take the interview seriously:

> Gass: There is a marvelously funny scene in the *Sot-Weed Factor*—
> Elkin: I read that passage and was very moved by it.

Gass: Oh Stanley is moved, moved, moved!
Elkin: I used to be a bowel.[2]

Elkin takes his amusement at the interview's expense, making flippant judgments, claiming to be moved to tears by passages, and uttering other nonsense—all of which is amusing, but reveals next to nothing about Elkin's work. Gass, by contrast, articulates the basis of his aesthetic: "As a writer I have only one responsibility, and that's to the language I'm using and to the thing I'm trying to make. Now as a person I have a lot of other responsibilities."[3] Gass has reiterated this view for most of his writing career and the statement cuts to the core of the fundamental distinction he draws between aesthetics and ethics. Gass makes no apologies for being a formalist of sorts, as he relates to Jan Garden Castro: "I'm interested in making a self-contained system of concepts, ideas that will then define a kind of consciousness.... It's not consciousness *of* the world; it's a consciousness *of* the work." And since he believes the literary object contains its own rules and structures, Gass is free to make art of anything, even that which is most sacred or profane. He further elaborates this idea to Richard Abowitz: "I don't think anything is sacred and therefore I am prepared to extol or make fun of anything. People who have very settled opinions are going to dislike this book [*The Tunnel*] because Kohler [*The Tunnel*] is the worm inside all of that stuff."

Further, says Gass to LeClair in a *Chicago Review* interview, "I want to get the reader to say yes to Kohler, although Kohler is a monster.... I want to give grandeur to a shit." Despite the fact that Gass wants a self-contained work that is not a window to the world, he also wants to lay bare the pettiness and meanness within us all: "Mainly I'm talking about the local holocausts, destruction of family. 'Fascism of the heart' is the phrase I use" (LeClair, *Chicago Review*). And this "fascism of the heart" is not an aberration of a twisted few he says to Heide Ziegler in *Anglistik:* "Kohler is not just an odd individual whom one can dismiss as a freak and a monster. Kohlers make up much of what mankind is."

"I think Plato was right, that poets do not tell the truth, that they persuade people through the emotions and the passions," Gass says in a *Modern Fiction Studies* interview. "So I have a moral point of view about fiction; namely its responsibility lies elsewhere, and if you think otherwise you're a sophist."[4] Although Gass denies that art should have a moral point and thus serve a social/political function, in his interview with Idiko Kaposi he implies that *The Tunnel*—his most ambitious, controversial, and complex work—has a

moral point at its core, which is that: Evil is ordinary; Kohler is ordinary; we
are Kohler.

Gass nevertheless self-consciously pushes the ethical limits of what readers will tolerate. Gass says, "but it's also true that one aim . . . is to challenge
those who say 'you can't write beautifully about some subjects; it's impossible, in fact immoral.'"[5] Such inclinations fueled the longstanding theoretical
debate between Gass and the late John Gardner, author of the influential *On
Moral Fiction,* who believed that fiction must not be made simply to be
beautiful. Unlike Gass, Gardner did not think that anything whatsoever can
be written about beautifully. Gardner, in speaking of the differences between
their respective fiction, says that "my 707 will fly and his is too encrusted
with gold to get off the ground" (LeClair, *New Republic*). Gass's retort is
that "what I really want is to have it sit there solid as a rock and have everyone think it is flying."

Not only does Gass push the limits of what is morally acceptable in fiction
he pushes the limits of traditional forms and genre. Gass wanted a condom
included with his novel *Willie Master's Lonesome Wife* so that one could
enter the text properly and safely. Gass believes in genre, he says, but only
to appropriate and violate them more effectively. He has published in a wide
array of genres, including collections of literary criticism (*Finding a Form,
The World Within the Word, Tests of Time*), philosophy (*On Being Blue*),
novels (*Willy Masters' Lonesome Wife, The Tunnel, Omensetter's Luck*), and
short story collections (*In the Heart of the Heart of the Country, Cartesian
Sonata*). His willingness to experiment in so many genres would seem to
bespeak his desire and ability to test the limits of language.

Gass, however, denies that the visual peculiarities or syntactical oddities
of his texts are new at all. We should always reach back, Gass explains to
Ronald Spatz, just as the moderns did, to discover the fundamentals of our
art, not merely to ape them or mindlessly distort them. "It would be quite a
challenge to just sit down and write a nice Victorian story," he comments.
"But, of course, there's no point in writing one that just passes back into the
past as if it had been written there. It has to be revivified, put to new uses."
In a later *Anglistik* interview with Ziegler, Gass echoes this sentiment while
denying that he is a postmodern writer: "Well, I do believe in genres, but I
believe in them because their rules can be occasionally violated with some
significance. . . . I've never been clear about the nature of postmodernism in
literature. I think a lot of people would call the book [*The Tunnel*] postmodern
because of the use of visuals, the presence of certain kinds of epistemological

difficulties, and my extensive use of quotation, but all those things have been done before. I think of my work as late or decayed modern."

In general, Gass would not have us read his works and adopt a new belief or change beliefs. Gass tells Janssens, "I have nothing I want to tell anybody . . . I have really no interest in persuading anybody. I have no sense of having something to tell somebody, and I suppose that is what I want to tell people." In a *Radical Imagination* interview with Ziegler, Gass reiterates this position: "Really, it is nice to cleanse yourself of beliefs. It is positively pleasant to find out that you do not need to believe nearly as many things as you thought you had to believe. It's a catharsis of the mind." And in a much later *Gadfly* interview with Abowitz, Gass is even more forceful: "I do not want anybody being influenced or following me. If I detected it I would drop the book in horror." One can hear in these remarks Gass's philosophical training in analytic philosophy, and even echoes of Pyrrhonian skepticism in which suspension of belief in order to achieve quietude is the goal of philosophizing.

Though much of Gass's central aesthetic has remained constant, there have been gradual shifts in his views on metaphor and ontology of the text. His view of metaphor is far more expansive than that proposed in the dissertation. Gass tells LeClair that "[m]etaphor has been thought to be a pet of language, a peculiar relation between subject and predicate . . . [b]ut you can make metaphors by juxtaposing objects and in lots of other ways" (*Paris Review*). In other words, metaphor need not be a purely linguistic matter, and perhaps not surprisingly Gass's change in his explanation of metaphor from graduate school to now signals a change in the focus of his fiction. As noted earlier Gass claims to construct self-contained systems of idead, but in these interviews, one can trace a growing concern with the relationship of his fiction to the world, as he makes clear to LeClair: "I've been principally interested in establishing the relationship between fiction and the world. If we can see that relationship as a metaphorical one, then we are already several steps in the direction of models."

But even while exploring that relation it is not so clear which side of the relation is more important. Consistent with his analytic training, Gass privileges the extra-linguistic world logically, even metaphysically, since there is no matter about which to write unless one first has experience. However, as Gass tells Spatz, "great texts have more reality than the things they're usually about. The situations the texts are about pass away; the texts remain and reoccur." Put differently to Kaposi, "texts do have a different kind of reality than the events they describe. . . . Ordinary events will be lost; their existence

as facts, their meaning, their significance will be lost if they're not reported."
Texts have a "different kind of reality." Gass accepts the more radical and
problematic view that even a fragmented work of art is more real than living
human beings. In a conversation with Arthur Saltzman in a *Contemporary
Literature* interview, Gass responds as follows:

> Saltzman: We've spoken before about the relative status in reality of historical
> and literary figures. Would you say that Huckleberry Finn is more "real" than,
> say, Alexander the Great because he is more fully realized in language?
> Gass: I certainly would.

Likewise in the *Chicago Review,* Gass responds to LeClair as follows, but
notice the difference:

> LeClair: You said once that a sentence can contain more being than a town.
> Have you changed . . .
> Gass: No. I am everyday more persuaded that that is the case. "More being" is
> rhetorical and designed to set the idea in motion against the opposition. The
> division that is commonly made between life on the one hand and literature on
> the other isn't tenable.

For Gass, the exploration of the relation of language and the world makes
no sense unless one accepts the reality of the two independently of one another, yet he also acknowledges that this independence is shifting sand. Without the linguistic representations, human experience and history slip into
memory and eventually fade away. The text may be all that remains of experience, but it is still an *account* and not the experience itself.

That is not to say Gass believes the text is all. In his view, there really is a
world "out there," certain things really did happen and history is not com-
petely malleable. According to Gass, the war for reality is a war of texts, and
some texts turn out more interesting, more important, more influential, and
more real that many people and also true that historical events cannot be
disputed. From Gass's standpoint, postmodernism thus fails us. While we
may write whatever we want, not every claim we call knowledge is a mere
verbal construct, nor subject to the scribbles of the pen. Zyklon B really does
kill, and we cannot rewrite chemistry so that it does not, nor construct a real
world in which it does not or did not.

Gass no longer argues that a work of fiction can be hermetically sealed,
but he still holds that his fundamental obligation as a writer is to the language

and he still says he does not want us to believe anything in particular after reading his books. Herein lies an unresolved paradox. He claims that his work is skeptical and uncommitted, and, as he quipped once in an aesthetics class at Washington University "my readers are lucky if I don't snip their noses off when I slam my books shut in their faces." On the other hand, says Gass to Kaposi, "The view I have is not that works of literature should not have ethical-political interests. It's impossible to exclude them, it's sort of crazy to." First, the problem, says Gass, is that "[a]rt is not the solution to everything. In fact, it solves hardly anything. It might make life bearable . . . [but] the more you tend to make you opinions artistically interesting, the less rhetorical effectiveness they tend to have" (Saltzman).

It may be difficult to see how Gass can claim that he has nothing he wants to tell anybody and also that he wants to lay bare the meanness of the world in his fiction. These interviews may help the reader decide whether Gass's non-postmodern skeptical bent really is manifest in his writing. The moral seriousness Gass brings to his work is difficult to reconcile with the claims that he wants to change no one's beliefs.

William Gass brings sentences to life and then tries to discern which direction the sentences flow and to what end. He creates, then must follow the creation, as he tells Jay White: "I always have to try to figure out from what I've done what should come next, and then I find out from looking at this lump that I cannot see anything that comes next. If I cannot see anything that comes next then I have to re-write what I've done until there is something that comes next. . . . I do that for ten years, and then maybe I've got a book done."

One may note in the recent interviews and his other recent writings a more obvious concern for social and political issues, such as the death sentence pronounced against Salman Rushdie: "I would like to see [the *fatwa*] reversed, of course, but we're dealing with governments. They want oil and they want power. They want to deal with Iran in a certain political way, and he's been sentenced to death. Who cares? As [President George (Sr.)] Bush said, 'He's just another author on a book tour.'"[6]

Gass champions no political theory, and would not have us change our beliefs after reading his fiction, but he certainly thinks that the measure of ignorance of society is how its writers are treated. But, of course, the freedom to write without risking a *fatwa* is insufficient. Even if we do not change a belief, our lives can become more tolerable through art created for the sake of itself, and through art created "to weaken the strength of the sacred text."[7]

According to Gass, the sacred texts of the world should be weakened because of the fanaticism they engender. "The world is pointless," Gass says flatly. "That's the thing that has to be faced. . . . My position is that life is meaningless. It's not a sign. We make meanings, but [life] does not."[8] Does Gass make meanings in his work and interviews? Perhaps, but they are not meanings, if we believe him, that he would have you believe.

I am much indebted to William Gass in ways too numerous to list but most importantly for agreeing to this project. And I am obviously indebted to the University Press of Mississippi for including this volume in the *Conversations* series, and especially to Seetha Srinivasan and Walter Biggins for their seemingly unlimited patience. I am indebted as well to Lorin Cuoco, former Associate Director of the International Writers Center at Washington University for access to crucial documents related to the book and for her constant good cheer, and to Michelle Komie, also formerly of the IWC, whose efficiency at finding non-existent addresses is unparalleled in the western world and who also tolerated (for a while) my silliness. Thanks much to all editors of all journals whose reprints appear here. And thanks finally, but not least to Lorie, Kristin, and Bethany for their love and joy.

TGA

Notes

1. William H. Gass, *Omensetter's Luck* (1966).
2. Stanley L. Duncan, "A Conversation for Stanley Elkin and William H. Gass," *The Iowa Review* (Winter 1976).
3. Ibid.
4. William T. Stafford, moderator, "A Colloquy with William H. Gass, with Brooke K. Korvath, Ruth H. Porritt, Martin D. Rapisarda, and Carol F. Richer," *Modern Fiction Studies* (Winter 1983: vol. 29, number 4).
5. Ibid.
6. William H. Gass and Lorin Cuoco, eds., *The Writer in Politics* (Southern Illinois University Press, 1996).
7. Richard Byrne, "Notes from Underground," *Riverfront Times* (Feburary 22–25, 1995).
8. Ibid.

Chronology

Heart of the Country" is included in *The Best American Short Stories of 1968*
Accepts full professorship in the Washington University (St. Louis) Philosophy Department
Marries Mary Alice Henderson

1970   Publishes *Fiction and the Figures of Life*

1973   *Chicago Tribune* Writers' and Critics' Poll: one of the ten best American writers. *Chicago Tribune* Writers' and Critics' Poll: one of the ten best Midwest writers

1975   American Academy and Institute of Arts and Letters Award for Fiction. Publishes *On Being Blue: A Philosophical Inquiry*

1978   Publishes *The World Within the Word*

1979   Awarded the David May Distinguished University Professorship in the Humanities, an endowed chair at Washington University. American Academy and Institute of Arts and Letters Medal of Merit for Fiction

1980   "The Old Folks" is included in *The Best American Short Stories of 1980*

1982   Elected to the American Academy of Arts and Sciences. Elected to the American Academy and Institute of Arts and Letters

1985   Publishes *The Habitations of the Word: Essays*

1990   Becomes director of the International Writers Center, Washington University

1995   Publishes *The Tunnel*

1996   Publishes *Finding a Form: Essays*. Wins American Book Award for *The Tunnel*

1997   National Book Critics Circle Award for Criticism for *Finding a Form: Essays*

1998   Publishes *Cartesian Sonata & Other Novellas*

1999   Publishes *Reading Rilke: Reflections on the Problems of Translation*

2000   Retires from Washington University and the International Writers Center

2002   Publishes *Tests of Time*

Conversations with William H. Gass

William H. Gass

Carole Spearin McCauley / 1971

From *The New Fiction: Interviews with Innovative American Writers,*
ed. Joe David Bellamy, University of Illinois Press, January 1974, 32–
44. Copyright by the Board of Trustees of the University of Illinois.
Used with permission of the University of Illinois Press.

Most philosophers don't write fiction. Or (if you're a cynic), fictions are all they write.

William Gass is both a philosopher who writes fiction and a writer whose aims and work have been deeply influenced by his philosophical training. His imaginative and experimental use of language and narrative technique in a variety of books has earned him both acclaim and dismissal during the years since parts of his first novel, *Omensetter's Luck,* appeared in *Accent Magazine.* About that book Susan Sontag wrote: "William Gass has written an extraordinary, stunning, beautiful book. I admire him and it very much." Richard Gilman remarked: "William Gass is not a comfortable writer. He's not immediately available. His work yields up new truths of our experience instead of repeating words of the past."

I began the following interview in late November, 1971, at the Poetry Center, YMHA, New York City, where Gass was reading. We completed it by mail over the next several weeks and months.

The following quotations are from *Fiction and the Figures of Life:*
". . . [H]ow absurd these views are which think of fiction as a mirror or a window onto life-as actually writing of living creatures . . ."
". . . [T]here are no events but words in fiction."
"The advantage the creator of fiction has over the moral philosopher is that the writer is concerned with the exhibition of objects, thoughts, feelings, and actions where they are free from the puzzling disorders of the real and the need to come to conclusions about them."

Carole Spearin McCauley: From your literary criticism (including the above) it seems the philosopher side of you mistrusts the fiction-writing side because the fiction process involves the deliberate telling of lies, the setting forth of actions and people that never happened. How do you reckon with this dilemma?

William Gass: I don't distrust the artist as artist at all. I distrust people, including artists, who make pretentious claims for literature, as a source of knowledge.

This was the half of Plato's complaint against the poets which I accept. I see no reason to regard literature as a superior source of truth, or even as a reliable source of truth at all. Going to it is dangerous precisely because it provides a sense of verification (a feeling) without the fact of verification (the validating process). Plato was simply too exclusive about his values. He took knowledge to be the supreme good. Consequently he had to banish the poets (for the most part). The appeal to literature as a source of truth is pernicious. Truth suffers, but more than that, literature suffers. It is taken to be an undisciplined and sophistic sociology, psychology, metaphysics, ethics, etc., etc. When I speak of telling lies, I speak ironically.

McCauley: It seems as if you desire your fictional characters to exist as pure essences, as ideas that the reader can apply to his own life, provided he doesn't assume they really exist beyond the page. For example, in *Fiction and the Figures of Life* (page 37) you say, "Though the handbooks try to tell us how to create characters, they carefully never tell us we are making images, illusions, imitations. Gatsby is not an imitation, for there is nothing he imitates." How did you arrive at this position, which puts you squarely against what most writers desire—and against all the advice to young writers to create "real characters in real situations"?

Gass: Most writers? Most writers of what sort? There is some truth to this, but it is also partly a myth about writers spread by critics and other advertisers who know nothing about the art of writing. "The only reality is the translation of one's ideas into rhythm and beautiful movements." Colette is a writer many would expect to be on an opposite side, but she isn't at all, and this is really true for most serious artists.

That advice to young writers—who is giving it? Teachers in writing workshops, journalists, editors, hacks. As a student of philosophy I've put in a great deal of time on the nature of language and belong, rather vaguely, to a school of linguistic philosophy which is extremely skeptical about the nature of language itself.

McCauley: In *Fiction and the Figures of Life* you find a "fear of feeling" in the work of some writers in our current literary pantheon such as Hawkes,

Barthelme, Coover, Barth, Nabokov, Borges—that they "neglect the full re-sponsive reach of their readers." So if you don't want the reader to "care" in the old sense of where-Hamlet-is-when-he's-not-onpage-or-onstage, then what is it exactly you want the reader to feel?

Gass: I want him to feel the way he feels when he listens to music—when he listens properly, that is. My complaint about Barth, Borges, and Beckett is simply that occasionally their fictions, conceived as establishing a meta-phorical relationship between the reader and the world they are creating, leave the reader too passive. But such words are misleading. I have little patience with the "creative reader."

I mean this: some metaphors work in one direction—the predicate upon the subject. When I say that her skin was like silk, I am using the concept silk, to interpenetrate and organize the idea of skin. Some metaphors, how-ever, interact—both terms are resonant. If Hardy writes, "She tamed the wildest flowers," then not only has "she" become an animal trainer, the flowers have become animals. Nor has "taming" been left untouched, for such taming is now seen in terms of gardening. Now if fictions are metaphors or models, then perhaps they should occasionally "fictionalize" the reader.

McCauley: In the words of Kohler, *The Tunnel's* narrator: "My subject's far too serious for scholarship, for history, and I must find another form before I let what's captive in me out. Imagine: history not serious enough, causality too comical, chronology insufficiently precise." Does fiction writ-ing interest you as the alternative? Like philosophy and Aristotle's "poetry," it can strive after the universal rather than the particular.

Gass: This is Kohler's problem, not mine. History, as I see it, can strive for the universal. My objection to it is simply that it rarely, reasonably, does. Many of my attitudes toward history are expressed by Levi-Strauss. For me fiction isn't an alternative to anything, however, and it doesn't strive for uni-versals. It merely makes particular things out of universals.

History, philosophy, fiction, like mathematics or physics, are for me all equally important, all difficult to do, rarely well done, each requiring its own disciplines, techniques, skills, and very different in aim. When Kohler says his subject is too serious for scholarship, etc., he means it is too personal, that the modes he mentions won't satisfy him. It reflects *his* mood.

McCauley: Wittgenstein defines philosophy as "a battle against the be-witchment of our intelligence by means of language." Does this relate to your concerns in fiction or philosophy?

Gass: I think philosophy is more than this, but it certainly should be this. It has often been busy bewitching. Philosophy ought to spend more time than it has showing how little we need it—it and other foolish sets of opinions. I believe much of what has passed for philosophy, theology, etc., in the past is nonsense. Sometimes beautiful nonsense, if you enjoy myths of the mind as I enjoy them. Beliefs are a luxury, and most of them are wicked gibberish.

Philosophical ideas can, however, provide the writer with complex centers of meaning, rich bases to work from. But you must *play* with them primarily because of the danger that what you're saying might be so. Constructing fictions as if the philosophy they're based on *were* so usually leads to falseness.

McCauley: How or where did you get the material for the characters and Ohio setting of *Omensetter's Luck?* For example, was Omensetter or Jethro Furber or the father in "The Pedersen Kid" modeled on someone you knew (who actually existed)?

Gass: I made it up. I know nothing whatever of Ohio river towns and care less. The only time I ever used a "model" in writing was when, as a formal device, and to amuse myself, I chose to get the facts about "B" in "In the Heart of the Heart of the Country" exactly right. Models interfere with the imagination. Which is better—to play train with a square wooden block, or a scale model? If you have a model, whether a person or a scene, even an idea, you tend to find yourself bent by that model when the work you are doing at any time should be obedient only to itself. Of course writers get ideas from models all the time and, occasionally, so do I, but they have to be able to leave the given behind. I generally take no chances and work "in the dark"— modelless.

Omensetter isn't really set in Ohio; that is the point.

McCauley: In your essay in *Afterwords: Novelists on Their Novels* you wrote, ". . . the illusion might wrap itself like a sheet around its occupant, so that Omensetter might become a ghost even to himself." Did you intend Omensetter to remain the mystery that many people find him—because we never got inside him directly?

Despite Omensetter's "luck," does his baby die?

Gass: Omensetter is a reflector. People use him the way they use their gods or other public figures—like ink blots—and upon them they project their hopes and fears. Who cared to know Omensetter? And when their hopes were dashed, they blamed the image in the mirror. So of course Omensetter is a mystery and he had to be left, in a sense, blank. Readers are now doing to him exactly what the characters in the book did.

No. His baby doesn't die. Omensetter is a lucky man.

McCauley: I notice a total difference in tone from something like passionate optimism (people's lives and deaths matter, America matters) in *Omensetter's Luck,* compared to the narrator's disenchantment in *The Tunnel.* How do you explain this?

Gass: The tonal difference is due to the differences in the books. The narrator in *The Tunnel* is disenchanted, but, again, that's his problem. I have always been disenchanted, although I am probably less bitter about things now than I was when I wrote *Omensetter's Luck.* I'm personally happier. But *The Tunnel* will be a very bitter book. I thought *Omensetter's Luck* pretty bitter, too. Also, you've only seen fragments from *The Tunnel.* If you saw more of it, your feeling about the tone might change.

McCauley: Do you feel America has lots its Omensetters, the people who know how to live naturally, unintellectually? Why or why not?

Gass: America never had its Omensetters. There aren't any such human felines. Such creatures are a part of the American myth. What we are losing is our belief in such things. Beliefs lost are minds cleaned. I applaud the development.

McCauley: You seem to have the kind of mind that brews fiction from massive amounts of stream of consciousness (Jethro Furber, Israbetis Tott). Do you have a method for keeping up the white heat, the Molly Bloom effect?

Gass: No method for "white heat." Whenever I find myself working at white heat, I stop until I cool off. I write very slowly, laboriously, without exhilaration, without pleasure, though with a great deal of tension and exasperation. I fuss over little bits, scarcely ever see beyond my nose, and consequently bump it constantly.

McCauley: Do you do much "research" to complete your fiction, make it real by revisiting "the scene of the crime," hunting out people who resemble your characters, etc?

Gass: No research. I collect words. Twelve different names for *whore* among the Romans. Thirty-five names for cloths and silk stuffs. Etc. Sometimes I even use what I've collected. Or an old book will suggest something. But there are no "scenes" to revisit, except for "B," and I wouldn't think of doing that while writing, because, as I said, my choice of factuality in that case was purely formal. I collected real names of clubs, for example, and amused myself by arranging them. Part of the game was not to invent any. It would have been like cheating at solitaire.

McCauley: Do you intend, as part of the fun, that the "Masters" in *Willie Masters' Lonesome Wife could* refer to William Masters of the St. Louis sex research? Or that "Kohler" in *The Tunnel* means "miner" in German?

Gass: I began *Willie* and wrote most of it in 1966, before I'd ever heard of Masters and Johnson. Scarcely before I'd ever heard of St. Louis. The jokes are there—in Goethe, in Shakespeare, etc.

The choice of "Kohler," however, was deliberate. Miner in the tunnel . . . yes.

McCauley: Do you have a writing schedule? Are you able to write every day? Do you do any sort of warmup exercises? What do you do if you get blocked?

Gass: I have a schedule for writing whenever I have enough free time that having such a schedule seems realistic—when I'm off because of a grant or during the summer. I used to be able to write nearly every day, but that has become impossible. I don't do warm-up exercises, but I do try to stop work only when I've left some fingers pointing to the future—some lines I can begin my next day's work by starting with. If I have to start cold, with entirely new material (new sentences, I mean), then I have trouble.

I don't really get blocked; that is, I don't find that I sit and stare at the page and nothing comes. Not for long. But I have blocks in the sense that I allow things to distract me so that for a long time I won't work. It is the same as a, block, though perhaps not so immediately distressing.

McCauley: Did you have to write for many years before you succeeded in being published?

Gass: I began writing seriously (I always wanted to write, planned on it, etc.) in 1951. I wrote "The Pedersen Kid" and the opening parts of *Omensetter* in '51–'52. I didn't get published until *Accent* devoted an issue to my work in 1958. *Omensetter* didn't get written for a long time, but it wasn't published until 1966. "The Pedersen Kid" (finished in '51) had to wait until 1961. Even *Willie* waited from 1966 to 68. "In the Heart" waited. They all wait. So that it is generally true that most of my stuff is old when it appears— old to me, that is.

McCauley: What do you like to read? Are there any authors you've learned something from?

Gass: I am an ominvorous reader. My library is that of a dedicated dilet-tante. I might, on any given day, be reading a book about bees, or about epistemology, or about the brain, or about the theory of signs, or about odd native tribes, or odd psychological states, or sexual positions, or who knows—travel, geography, biography. . . . I like letters, diaries, journals, gossip, and therefore history. I read less and less poetry, though I get to Rilke almost every day. I rarely read fiction and generally don't enjoy it. I usually read it because I have to. Lately, most of my reading has been of that sort. I read X because I have to shoot off my mouth about it—teaching, reviewing— and I'm sick of it.

I've learned from so many I couldn't even begin to list the essential. As far as my own writing goes, from poets mostly, from philosophers, of course, because they supply me with material, and from stylists in general, whether Sir Thomas Browne, Hobbes, Stein, Joyce, James, Ford, or Colette.

McCauley: Do you enjoy any of the other arts?

Gass: I enjoy all of them, especially perhaps ballet (when pure and not mucked up) and architecture. I was an opera nut when young. That's tailed off. I haunt museums when I can. In one sense, painting has influenced my theory of art more than almost anything, music my practice of it.

McCauley: Do you write poetry or plays?

Gass: I wrote terrible poetry in my youth. I write doggerel now. I am a rotten poet and have absolutely no talent for it.

I haven't the dramatic imagination at all. Even my characters tend to turn away from one another and talk to the void. This, along with my inability to narrate, is my most serious defect (I think) as a writer and incidentally as a person. I am (though I wasn't especially raised as one) a Protestant, wholly inner-directed, and concerned only too exclusively with *my* salvation, *my* relation to the beautiful, *my* state of mind, body, soul. . . . The interactions which interest me tend to be interactions between parts of my own being. One could, I suppose, try to get a little drama out of that. Besides, the drama is a mug's game. Actors are enemies. The theater is cheap, divided in its source of control. It would drive me crazy.

McCauley: Do political issues on campus or among students interest you for their fictional possibilities? That is, there's terrible pressure on fiction to "be relevant" today, to deal with "today's real issues" instead of rural people or private consciousness. So we have Norman Mailer making his career as a sort of hippy-fascist weathercock telling us how tomorrow's winds will blow in America. How do you deal with this pressure to "be relevant"?

Gass: Art is never concerned with such things. Relevance is meaningless to it. A work of art is made to last as a valuable being in the world. As such it may develop, over time, useful relations to the world; but just as human beings ultimately must find their values in themselves, so works of art must *be relevant by being.* There have always been Mailers because culture requires its human talismans. These procedures and activities are as different from art as weeds from differential equations. I feel no pressure to be relevant.

I am, of course, as a person, interested in these public matters, and I am frequently taken from my work to engage in them. They are, indeed, often far more important than myself and my private playthings. Dante was "relevant," but fortunately he triumphed over it.

McCauley: Is teaching a stimulus to your writing, or something that just takes time from it? I know that you received the Hovde Prize for excellence in teaching in 1967.

Gass: It used to be. I think I fed on the students. They have been an enormous help to me in every way, but my interest in teaching grows less—I think mainly because my toleration of the monkey business which attends it grows less. Now I often feel that it just takes time. But I really enjoy lecturing (not teaching); I never really enjoyed teaching. I enjoy talking to the material. And if I'm not doing that aloud, I'm doing it silently. It's nice to get paid for it.

McCauley: Someone from the Midwest (even New Jersey!) can feel discriminated against by the New York literary establishment, perhaps criticized for being provincial, unsophisticated, whatever. Has this kind of treatment ever afflicted you?

Gass: When I go to New York City, I feel I'm going to the provinces. What is sophisticated about literary New York? How much of importance goes on there? It is filled with commercial hacks and their pimps. There are, of course, many cultivated people—people who have their values straight, who know even more about Valéry or Péguy, say, than about Mailer or Updike—but most of them mistake the literary froth for the body of the beer.

Literature doesn't take place in New York. It takes place in writers' heads and on their pages all over the world. From the literary point of view New Yorkers live in the servants' quarters. No, I haven't been afflicted. Literature is where the Faulkners are. No Faulkner is in New York, and if he were, he wouldn't be known. I snub them.

McCauley: Did you have to submit *Omensetter's Luck* to many publishers before it was noticed by New American Library and other people in New York?

Gass: I think *Omensetter's Luck* went to twelve publishers (so much for New York sophistication). New American Library didn't notice it. It takes no notice of books. David Segal saw the book early on—tried to get it published at McGraw-Hill, finally succeeded at NAL. If it hadn't been for my agent, Lynn Nesbit, and for David, it probably would still be unpublished, and so would all the rest of my stuff.

McCauley: Did they suggest or require many revisions?

Gass: David suggested a few revisions—nothing major—most wise suggestions from him. I do my own work and do not permit other people to interfere with it. Editors occasionally ask for cuts, and sometimes I submit to them (for magazine publication). Anyone who requires revisions has simply rejected the manuscript as far as I'm concerned. Some (a few) wanted to do that with *Omensetter's Luck.*

McCauley: How do you generally revise your work? Just two drafts or many more?

Gass: I work not by writing but by rewriting. Each sentence has many drafts. Eventually there is a paragraph. This gets many drafts. Eventually there is a page. This gets many drafts. And so on. I have about three hundred pages of *The Tunnel.* But in a few days I start over redrafting them—from the beginning.

Writing isn't easy for me. That's why I have to answer your questions in pidgin, for if I began to worry about what I was saying and the way I was saying it—well, I'd never answer your questions. I would never emerge from number one: So I'm a poor correspondent. I deliberately butcher manners. Write wretchedly. Turn no phrases. Speak telegraphese.

McCauley: How do you feel about *The Tunnel* compared with *Omensetter's Luck?* Progression or enlargement?

Gass: *The Tunnel* is a crucial work for me. All my work up to it I have privately thought of as exercises and preparations. This was a dodge, of course, but it did work. How can you fail when you are simply practicing, learning, experimenting? I can't hide behind that dodge any more. Further, in this business it is no honor to finish second. Now I shall find out whether I am any good.

Certainly I hope that *The Tunnel* will be better than *OL*. *OL* made compromises. I trust that *The Tunnel* will not. I hope that it will be really original in form and in effect, although mere originality is not what I'm after.

OL made compromises because it still sometimes treated fiction as if it were an imitation of some factual form. *OL* made only sporadic steps at establishing its own form.

Fiction has traditionally and characteristically borrowed its forms from letters, journals, diaries, autobiographies, histories, travelogues, news stories, backyard gossip, etc. It has simply *pretended* to be one or other of them. The history of fiction is in part a record of the efforts of its authors to create for fiction its own forms. Poetry has its own. It didn't borrow the ode from somebody. Now the novel is imagined news, imagined psychological or sociological case studies, imagined history . . . feigned, I should say, not imagined. As Rilke shattered the journal form with *Malte,* and Joyce created his own for *Ulysses* and *Finnegan,* I should like to create mine.

McCauley: Do you have any advice for beginning writers? Do you recommend fiction writing classes? Would you ever teach creative writing? If so, what would be your approach?

Gass: My advice for beginning writers is first to recognize that writers differ a great deal in their own natures and in the nature of their talent, and that little advice which is general can be of much value. Learn not to take advice. Look to yourself. Make yourself worthy of trust.

No art can be taught, though some techniques sometimes can. Writing classes help some, don't others. It depends again on the kind of person you are. Do whatever works. It wouldn't have worked for me, and I am personally suspicious of them. I've taught creative writing (a little), but I would never make a habit of it. All that attention wasted on poor work? Better to speak of the good things and learn from that. So my approach would be flight.

McCauley: Can you estimate when your book *The Tunnel will* be finished or published?

Gass: I began *The Tunnel* in 1966. I imagine it is several years away yet. Who knows, perhaps it will be such a good book no one will want to publish it. I live on that hope.

An Interview with William Gass

Gary Mullinax / 1972

From *Delaware Literary Review,* 1.1 (Spring 1972), 81–87. Reprinted by permission.

William Gass is highly regarded as both an author and a critic. Roger Shattuck has compared Gass's fiction to that of James Joyce, while Geoffrey Wolff in *Newsweek* has said of his critical work: "For anyone who writes fiction, or writes about it, or reads fiction . . . Gass's book is the most important and bracing theoretical study that I know of."

Gary Mullinax: I want to discuss primarily your theories about contemporary fiction. Maybe a good place to start is a quotation from one of your essays in which you say, about Malcolm Lowry's *Under the Volcano,* that "few novels are so little like life, few are so formal and arranged, there are few whose significance is so total and internal." This seems to lead to the notion that many recent critics have of contemporary fiction as conscious artifice, a movement away from realism. Do you see this kind of thing as the dominant trend among good contemporary writers?

Gass: Yes, I do. The ones at any rate whom I call good contemporary writers—it's a self-selective kind of thing, I guess, in the sense that I tend to see those people as good who are doing that kind of thing. I think it's very much a preoccupation with most of the writers—not all, but most—whom I admire. And they are engaged in it almost with a kind of Messiah feeling about it. They're not just doing it. They're actually kind of preaching it in the work—forcing it on the reader. So there's a great deal of pedagogy to it too. The works aren't just standing there by themselves. They're in a sense saying, "I'm standing here by myself. Look, I'm just standing here all by myself." And this is really rather odd, because in one sense it's defeating what they're saying they're doing: not teaching.

Mulinax: Teaching the reader that they're not trying to teach him anything?

Gass: Right.

Mullinax: What writers do you have in mind here?

Gass: Well, I think Barthelme does this quite a lot. I think Robert Coover is presently very much engaged in this kind of thing. Barth also. Borges, of course, from whom I suppose a lot of this stems. Beckett doesn't do that kind of instructional bit, but he's very much in that general mode.

Mullinax: Why do you think the realistic or conventional, traditional novel is not being written by our better writers? Do you see it as a cultural thing? Do you think it inevitable that the realistic novel decline and this new kind of fiction gain the upper hand?

Gass: Oh I don't think it will gain the upper hand in the sense of dominating the consciousness of very many people. I think fiction is going the way of poetry. It's getting increasingly technical, increasingly more aimed at a small audience, and so forth. And this is what happened to poetry—over a long period of time. And now fiction, which I suppose was once the leading popular art form, certainly isn't any more. And serious fiction does not even hope for it. I think what may happen more and more, however, is what has already started to happen in fiction—a loss of linearity, a tendency to get away from storytelling, character development, and so on. This has been taken over by the movies, of course, in lots of ways. But I think that sort of thing is characteristic of a lot of modern consciousness. So in a curious way the novel, by becoming less and less linear and less and less oriented in the traditional way, may be becoming more and more realistic.

Mullinax: Does the kind of fiction you have been describing correspond to your notion of what good fiction should be; is it the best of all possible fictions?

Gass: Well, I think these happen to be the best writers now. I don't mean that somebody couldn't turn around and write a great "traditional" novel.

Mullinax: So we could have another Tolstoy?

Gass: Sure. And then of course Barth is a great master of narrative form. I don't suppose there's been a person with such skill as a narrator, storyteller in the old sense, as he is. Incredible. But he doesn't use that gift in the same way at all. No, I think that it just happens that the people I think have the greatest abilities are doing this kind of thing.

Mullinax: What do you see as the value to the reader of this kind of art? The kind of art that doesn't, at least on the surface, comment on life, doesn't do anything. A consciously artificial art.

Gass: I think it constructs new consciousness. Suppose, for instance, you're listening to a piece of music, and you're really listening to it. Then in a sense you've blocked out of consciousness your existence in every other respect but that music. Since really all we are in a way at any time is our consciousness, if you've replaced your consciousness with Mozart or something, and you're really concentrating, following that music—not woolgathering, just listening, hard—you're nothing but that music. Well what that's done is create a consciousness that's—in this case—totally auditory, which you couldn't get by having an experience anywhere in the world, because you can't go out and "hear" Mozart in nature. And it is an experience—a thing, sound—constructed entirely to be heard, for the sole purpose of being heard, for the sole purpose of capturing your consciousness, for the purpose of being yourself at that time. And this can be an electrifying experience because it's a consciousness that's entirely new, completely non-natural, and better than anything you could imagine for yourself. Now a work of fiction is a construction of a verbal world through which the reader passes, in which he becomes immersed in the way that he does when he's listening to a piece of music. And this gives you a world which doesn't have to be anything like the world outside. Why?! I mean if you can go out and see these things and hear and feel them then you don't need to have words do it. But the words— just like the music—do things you can't get in nature. And it can be a really electrifying change in your consciousness.

Mullinax: This of course gets to the notion of fiction as a separate world, and not as an appendage of some sort to the "real" world. The idea that we should let fiction be fiction, and not philosophy or sociology or psychology.

Gass: Right. We've allowed music to be music. Oh we try, of course, to make it out to be something else. We use music in a roundabout way. Music to make love by, all that stuff. But we don't normally go around regarding music as anything more than music, and not as a message to the world or this or that. And we're doing that more and more with poetry. Fiction is slower to get there because it's been attached to doing all these other things. Art shouldn't try to make you do something, or even to produce in the reader a feeling or emotion. Its aim is construction. The artist wants to create an object that has intrinsic value, something worth living with as an end in itself. The artist makes an object he can have a non-utilitarian relation to—a companion.

Mullinax: Do you see as one of the values of conscious artifice the demonstration of what a writer can do in terms of coming to terms with his material?

Gass: That's certainly a value. It's part of the value we find in other things too. In sports, for example. Mastery. The ability to do certain things, even if they're absurd. In a way, it's intrinsically absurd to take a long pole and hurl yourself over a high bar. Or to hit a little ball a long way and drop it into a small cup. Yet this is mastery. So the actual display of virtuosity which we have a good deal of in modern fiction is partly this too. And there is an esthetic relationship between sports and art.

Mullinax: Robert Scholes discusses the idea that many writers are more certain esthetically than before and less certain ethically. Do you see in contemporary authors the assertion "Don't trust me too far; I'm having a lot of fun with this but . . ."

Gass: Yes, constantly in fact undercutting themselves and saying, over and over, "Well look, this is only a fiction." For one thing they don't trust their values the way novelists used to. But this also allows them to make assertions which they would be embarrassed to make otherwise. It's like thinking up a clever remark and being embarrassed to say it, but then attributing it to somebody else. So a lot of the time feelings, attitudes, and so on, which they would really be embarrassed to express—afraid they'd be thought square or naive—they can get across that way.

Mullinax: How about Barth's notion of the Literature of Exhaustion, the idea that literary forms have been used up and that contemporary writers of necessity turn back to past literary conventions and use them in effect as subject matter? Do you agree that this is a major motivation of much contemporary fiction?

Gass: Yes. I think the materials that previous writers used were often things they experienced in their ordinary lives, things in the street and so forth. But of course we're library bred now. Now the things that are most intimate for writers are other books. The biggest experience often in writers' lives is reading *Don Quixote* or something. So instead of talking about your love affair when you were young you, talk about your love affair with *Don Quixote*. And the forms of all these become the material you want to work with.

Mullinax: Do you as a writer of fiction feel that the literary forms are used up, that everything has been done?

Gass: No. It's as if nothing had happened. There's no barrier at all.

William Gass: The Art of Fiction LXV

Thomas LeClair / 1976

From *The Paris Review,* 70 (1977), 61–94. Reprinted by the permission of Russell & Volkening as agents for *The Paris Review.* Copyright © 1977 by *The Paris Review.*

In the book-bound alcove off the bare room where he writes when at home, William Gass gave this interview in July of 1976. Sitting in cut-offs and T-shirt, sipping on a bottle of Ballantine ale, Gass resembles a boyish headmaster at his Sunday ease. When he talks the small shifts of his compact body, the voice's inflections, and the mind's dartings reveal a writer harsh on himself and his work, though generous in his responses.

Now 53, Gass is professor of philosophy at Washington University in St. Louis. His books are: *Omensetter's Luck,* a novel (1966); *In the Heart of the Heart of the Country,* stories (1968); *Fiction and the Figures of Life,* essays (1970); *Willie Masters' Lonesome Wife,* a fictional essay (1971); and *On Being Blue,* criticism (1976). Parts of *The Tunnel,* his novel in progress, have been appearing since 1969.

Interviewer: Do you feel you are writing full throat now?

Gass: I hope so, but if I am a hound, at what am I baying? I am basically a closet romantic, a tame wild man. When I was in college I closed the closet door behind me. Then, for all sorts of reasons, some artistic if you like, but at bottom personal as bottoms are, I became a formalist: I became detached; I emphasized technique; I practiced removal. I was a van. I took away things. And I became a toughie, a hardliner. When I was in High School, I chanted Thomas Wolfe and burned as I thought Pater demanded and threatened the world as a good Nietzschean should. Then at college, in a single day, I decided to change my handwriting . . . which meant, I realized later, a change in the making of the words which even then were all of me I cared to have admired. It was a really odd decision. Funny. Strange. I sat down with the greatest deliberation and thought how I could make each letter of the alphabet from that moment on. A strange thing to do. Really strange. And for years I carefully wrote in this new hand—I wrote everything: marginal notes, reminders, messages—in a hand that was very Germanic and stiff. It had a certain artificial elegance, and from time to time I was asked to address wedding invitations, but when I look at that hand now I am dismayed, if not a little frightened, it is so much like strands of barbed wire. Well, that change of script was a response to my family situation and in particular to my parents. I fled an emotional problem and hid myself behind a wall of arbitrary formality. Nevertheless, I think that if I eventually write anything which has any enduring merit, it will be in part because of that odd alteration. I submitted myself to a comparatively formal, rather rigorous, kind of philosophical training. I stuffed another tongue in my mouth. It changed my tastes. It wasn't Shelley any longer, it was Pope. It wasn't even Melville, it was James. Most of these changes were for the better because, being a little older, I saw more in my new choices than I had in my old ones. But now, after maybe 20 years of not going near Nietzsche—of even being embarrassed by my youthful enthusiasms—I find him exciting again. My handwriting has slowly relaxed and now the sloppy kindergarten scrawl I had as a child. I suspect the same kind of thing is happening in my work. I am ready to go in any direction. But I hope I've learned that the forms are inherent, that the formal discipline is inherent, so that when I want to start improvising I won't have forgotten how to dance. It wasn't until I was ready to come out of my formal phase that I began to read Rilke. Once I took my thumb out of my mouth—well—soon there was no dike. So now I try to manage two horses: there is one called Valéry and another called Rilke. I remember I once compared writing to the image of the charioteer in the *Phaedrus*. Intellectually, Valéry is still the person I admire most among artists I admire most; but when it comes to the fashioning of my own work now, I am aiming at a Rilkean kind of celebrational object, thing, *Dinge*.

Interviewer: How much did this change have to do with your family?

Gass: I think a lot of it was deeply personal. Every powerful reason is a cause, accounts for a condition. When you decide to change your handwriting, and when you sit down and spend a day or more making new characters, you've got to be in an outraged and outrageous state of mind. I simply rejected my background entirely. I decided, as one of my characters says, to pick another cunt to come from. Did I come out of that hole in the wallpaper, Rilke has his hero, Malte, wonder. I just had to make myself anew—or rather, *seem* to. So I simply started to do it. And I think it very obvious now though it wasn't obvious to me then, that I should pick the way I formed words to be the point where I should try to transform everything. The alphabet, for

Christ's sake—I would have changed that, if I'd been able. So all along one principal motivation behind my writing has been to be other than the person I am. To cancel the consequences of the past. I am not the person who grew up in some particular place, though people try to label me as a local Midwestern writer; but I never had roots; all my sources (as a writer) were chosen. I chose to be influenced by this or that book or chose to be defined as the author of this or that. I think that for a long time I was simply emotionally unable to handle my parents' illnesses. My mother was an alcoholic and my father was crippled by arthritis and his own character. I just fled. It was a cowardly thing to do, but I simply would not have survived. I still hate scenes unless I make them. My situation certainly wasn't more severe than most people endure at some time in their lives, but I was not equipped to handle it. What is perhaps psychologically hopeful is that in *The Tunnel* I am turning back to inspect directly that situation and that means I haven't entirely rejected it. On the other hand, I am taking a damn long time to write the book. But I don't know. What is psychologically best for a writer is what produces his best work. I suspect that in order for me to produce my best work I have to be angry. At least I find that easy. I am angry all the time.

Interviewer: Have you spent a good part of your writing life getting even?

Gass: Yes . . . yes. Getting even is one great reason for writing. The precise statement of the motive is tricky; but the clearest expression of my unwholesome nature and my mean motives (apart from trying to write well) appears in a line I like in "In the Heart of the Heart of the Country." The character says "I want to rise so high that when I shit I won't miss anybody." But maybe I say it's a motive because I like the line. Anyway, my work proceeds almost always from a sense of aggression. And usually I am in my best working mood when I am, on the page, very combative, very hostile. That's true even when I write to praise, as is often the case. If I write about Colette, as I am now, my appreciation will be shaped by the sap-tongued idiots who don't perceive her excellence. I also take considerable pleasure in giving obnoxious ideas the best expression I can. But getting even isn't necessarily vicious. There are two ways of getting even: one is destructive and the other is restorative. It depends on how the scales are weighted. Justice, I think, is the word I want.

Interviewer: Isn't there a line in *Willie Masters' Lonesome Wife* about the pencil moving against the page with anger?

Gass: Something like that. sure. I am developing a theory about that in an essay I'm writing on creativity. One doesn't want to generalize from what might be just a private psychology, but it seems to me the emotion is central. There is another sentence from *Willie* that should be mentioned here, though: "how close in the end is a cunt to a concept; we enter both with joy." That's the other line of mine I remember with pleasure. And both express something very close to me. If someone asks me, "Why do you write?" I can reply by pointing out that it is a very dumb question. Nevertheless there is an answer. I write because I hate. A lot. Hard. And if someone asks me the inevitable next dumb question. "Why do you write the way you do?" I must answer that I wish to make my hatred acceptable because my hatred is much of me, if not the best part. Writing is a way of making the writer acceptable to the world—every cheap dumb nasty thought, every despicable desire, every noble sentiment, every expensive taste. There isn't very much satisfaction in getting the world to accept and praise you for things that the world is prepared to praise. The world is prepared to praise only shit. One wants to make sure that the complete self, with all its qualities, is not just accepted but approved . . . not just approved—whoopeed.

Interviewer: Did your years at Kenyon College have much influence on your later aesthetic positions?

Gass: Not directly. I was already very fascinated by Ransom's stuff when I was in high school. I wrote an article on Ransom and sent it to him at the *Kenyon Review.* It was godawful, but he was very sweet and returned it with a nice letter. I'd never met him, but I was so in love with the man's "manner" I scrawled his initials in the books of his I owned and pretended to others that he'd signed them. When I got to Kenyon he did remember my essay, or was polite enough to pretend to. And that "manner" was real. When I was going to school there, the faculty were very much under the influence of Ransom and the New Criticism, but I think that influence was so widespread you'd have found it most places. I did audit a few courses that Ransom taught, but I didn't take any courses in English while I was at Kenyon. I was busy taking philosophy and other things of that sort. And I found that I fought English classes. I was such a smartass I thought I knew much more than the instructor. No, my pretentions got ground beneath another heel. I couldn't get published in the literary magazine—not a colorful fart, not a thumbprint. The students were very good writers; some of them were publishing in the *Review* already. And I held a small limp pen; I was terrified and crushed; I couldn't get anywhere; I was unbelievably bad; I was lousy. I knew the for-

malist ideas were in the air, of course, but I didn't really come face to face
with them in any extensive way until I went to grad school, so I think that
the influence of Kenyon was predominantly philosophical.

Interviewer: What was your orientation when you were working on your
Ph.D. in philosophy at Cornell?

Gass: I wanted to work in aesthetics, but they didn't have anybody who
was interested in the area, and I didn't take any courses in the subject. They
had a nice elderly man the students called "Bedsprings" because he rocked
from his toes to his heels all the time and stared at the girls. Most of my
courses were in language analysis, philosophy of science, logic, and the theory of meaning. The faculty finally settled on allowing me one wild paper a
year which they would be agreeable about and not grade. What I eventually
ended up doing was working with the philosophy of language and the theory
of metaphor with Max Black. I had to learn to write analytical stuff for all
those people, and it is not my natural manner. I hated it in lots of ways
because I was working against the grain all the time. But it was very good
for me. It was a superb faculty.

Interviewer: Do you still retain that rigor?

Gass: I can still use it, though it isn't easy. I still admire it. I hope I can
recognize its many fakes. Now I don't have to be what one would call "rigorous" very often any more except in some classroom situations, because when
I'm writing I find it very difficult to harmonize a desire for a certain kind of
style with the rigor and precision appropriate to a certain kind of subject. The
only compromise I can manage is expressed by the hope that I've done a
reasonably thorough job on any philosophical issue before I start to write, so
that beneath that fluffy flamboyant style and all that sweet sugary rhetoric
there is some real cake—some sense at least of the complications of the
problem. But I don't pretend to be treating issues in any philosophical sense.
I am happy to be aware of how complicated, and how far from handling
certain things properly I am, when I am swinging so wildly around.

Interviewer: It seems that the style no matter how flamboyant is always
very precise.

Gass: Well, I hope so, and you are a kind person to suggest it. Rigor is
achieved by pushing things very hard and trying to uncover every possible
ramification, nuance, and aspect, and then ordering those things very, very
carefully. I think that's always valuable. Still, the kind of ordering you get in

philosophy is quite different from the kind you try for in literature, although there is a similarity—an analogy. That's one of the reasons why I admire mathematicians, I guess. You found beauty listening to Austin give a lecture—he presented a beautiful landscape of the mind. Everything was so crisp and beautifully drawn. It was like watching a good draftsman. It wasn't as profound or original as Wittgenstein, for instance, but it was really a pleasure to hear such a careful disposal of ideas: a trash bag anybody'd be happy to plug on TV.

Interviewer: Is Austin's and Searle's notion of speech acts of any use to you as a writer?

Gass: If you start talking about speech acts, what you are doing is connecting the notion of writing with a concept of performance. I think contemporary fiction is divided between those who are still writing performatively and those who are not. Writing for voice, in which you imagine a performance in the auditory sense going on, is traditional and old fashioned and dying. The new mode is not performative and not auditory. It's destined for the printed page, and you are really supposed to read it the way they teach you to read in speed reading. You are supposed to crisscross the page with your eye, getting references and gists; you are supposed to see it flowing on the page, and not sound it in the head. If you do sound it, it is so bad you can hardly proceed. It can't all have been written by Dreiser, but it sounds like it. *Gravity's Rainbow* was written for print, *JR* was written by the mouth for the ear. By the mouth for the ear; that's the way I'd like to write. I can still admire the other—the way I admire surgeons, broncbusters, and tight ends. As writing, it is that foreign to me.

Interviewer: But in *Willie Masters' Lonesome Wife* . . .

Gass: Oh, sure, there I'm playing around with it. . . . Yes, I was trying out some things. Didn't work. Most of them didn't work. I was trying to find a spatial coordinate to go with the music, but my ability to manipulate the spatial and visual side of the medium was so hopelessly amateurish (I was skating on one galosh), and the work also had to go through so many hands, that the visual business was only occasionally successful, and most of that was due to the excellent design work of Larry Levy, not me. Too many of my ideas turned out to be only ideas—situations where the reader says: "Oh yeah, I get the idea," but that's all there is to get, the idea. I don't give a shit for ideas—which in fiction represent inadequately embodied projects—I care only for affective effects. I'm still fooling around with visual business, but I am thinking of a way to make them *sound.* One problem, for instance, is trying to get the sense (in print) of different lines of language being sounded at the same time, or alternately, or at different speeds or pitch, as in music.

Interviewer: You've said that the love of the world as a resonance or shape is the least understood of all aesthetic phenomena.

Gass: One of the things which children do early on is discover the ability they have to surround themselves with their own sensory world. Shit, piss, and bellow, kick and wiggle: that's it! I think that what often makes writers is a continued sense of the marvelous palpable quality of making words and sounding them. My god how Beckett has it. I have a very strong feeling about that love of making sounds. I think it must have been very enjoyable—in the old days—to form letters with your quill or pen and hand. I, for example, still have an old typewriter. An electric takes away from the expressiveness of the key. It was very important for Rilke to send a copy of the finished poem in his beautiful hand to somebody, because *that was* the poem, not the printed imitation. Writing by hand, mouthing by mouth: in each case you get a very strong physical sense of the emergence of language—squeezed out like a well-formed stool—what satisfaction!—what bliss! That's another reason why I like the metaphor, in *Willie Masters',* of cunt and concept. As an artist you are dealing with a very abstract thing when you are dealing with language (and if you don't realize that, you miss everything) yet suddenly it is there in your mouth with great particularity—drawl, lisp, spit. When the word passes out into the world that particularly is ignored; print obliterates it; type has no drawl. But if you can write for that caressing, slurring, foul mouthed singing drunken voice . . . that's a miracle. Gertrude Stein said poetry was caressing nouns, and I think she was right, only I wouldn't leave out verbs or prepositions, articles or adverbs, anything. . . .

As a writer you are, of course, aware of the arbitrary relationship of symbol-sounds to their meanings; but no real writer wants it that way. In doing *On Being Blue,* I was struck by the way in which meanings are historically attached to words: it is so accidental, so remote, to twisted. A word is like a schoolgirl's room—a complete mess—so the great thing is to make out a way of seeing it all as ordered, as right, as inferred and following. Now when you take language out of the realm in which it is produced and put it in poetry and fiction, you transform it completely. Maybe that is the least understood aesthetic phenomenon. That process of transformation is perhaps the essence of creative activity. And if you take really bowel turning material, from the point of view of its pragmatic importance in the world; and surround it like kitty litter with stuff that is there purely for play, then you can get an electric line between the two poles clothes would turn white simply hanging on. The electricity of Elizabethan drama is total. They are talking always of life and death matters, but they are standing there playing with their mouths.

Interviewer: Do you sound words over and over to yourself at the typewriter?

Gass: Yes. One time, two times, three times, times, times, times. . . . That's the final test. When that goes well, all's well—well, nearly all's well. And it stands. A bad line or a missed start will get scratched down so deeply in my head like a schoolkid's desk he's trying to carve 'fuck,' 'cunt,' and his name on, that it becomes extremely hard for me to start over and go at the sentence in a different way. I am almost never able to do that. If I've a botch at the beginning, I have to keep fiddling around until I have somehow fiddled it into a squeak, the squeak into the score. This damn imprinting is one of the hardest things I have to overcome. But I also appreciate Valéry's account of how a poem came to him because and while he was walking the meter. When work is going well for me—which is rarely—I have a clear metrical sense of sound and pace. This whole problem is vital. When one section is singing, it sings the rest. I've heard many of the speeches in Elkin that way. The song began and sang itself. Prose gives you flexibility, and you want to use it to shift the whole mode or manner of voice within a paragraph or within a single sentence. So you must have a notion, some clues, which will do the job. Joyce fiddled around with a lot of things trying to get that done, but I didn't get those clues of his until I heard him on records. Then I realized how he should be sung and that he had in mind a notation which isn't present in the book.

One problem is that the reader isn't conditioned, hasn't the time, intelligence, patience, to perform the work. When you think of being a good reader, you tend to think of yourself or somebody as having a sharp eye, quick intelligence, who pays attention, follows this resonance of meaning or that, and has a good memory for what happened before, and all that admirable true crap. But who thinks of the reader as an oral interpreter? When I read a traditional novel, I never remember anything except language, the rhythms in the language patterns, and I do have a good memory for that. I think I forgot the basic plot of *Middle—march* [sic] hours after I read it, and it was of course a terrific book. But the impression, the quality of its style, that I think

I shall remember forever. One used to read Henry James aloud. It's the only way to read him. But it takes time; you've got to figure out how to do it, and all this alters the temporal reach of the work entirely. Beckett is our best example. You look at the text and you see all those pauses. You say to yourself, yes, there are pauses, but you don't pause. You don't perform it. If you don't perform it, you ain't got it. In music, you can't *think* the rests, pretend the silences. There happen to be some splendid Beckett manuscripts at Washington University, and they taught me a great deal. I went over a little story called "Ping" one day with the idea of reading it aloud. It's about six or seven pages, but it is a half an hour or more in the reciting. If you do it properly, well spaced, larded with silence, then it's overpowering. You gotta wait, you know, and wait, and wait, and wait, and we just don't do that sort of thing—the world turns—who has time to wait between two syllables for just a little literary revelation? A lot of modern writers, I remember saying, are writing for the fast mind that speeds over the text like those noisy bastards in motor boats. The connections are all spatial and all at various, complicated, intellectual levels. They stand to literature as fast food to food.

Interviewer: Have you considered giving the reader some kind of extra textual directions on how to read as Barth does in *Lost in the Funhouse?*

Gass: "The Pedersen Kid" has some. *Willie* is full of them. I keep fussing around, trying to find ways to symbolize what I want. But notation . . . notation . . . what a difficulty! The myth is that Joyce tried to indicate that the speed passages in *Finnegan's Wake* should be taken by variously spacing the words. In the novel I'm working on now, I want, for instance, a certain word to sound like a bell the whole time the reader is reading certain lines. I want this bong going bong all the bonging time. I'm trying to figure out what device will work—on the page—not only to give the proper instruction to the reader, but make him begin to hear it—dead dead dead dead—the way it's supposed to go. But as soon as you try to note it the page goes crazy and you get a dozen other things you want no part of.

Interviewer: Is the reader an adversary for you?

Gass: No. I don't think much about the reader. Ways of reading are adversaries—those theoretical ways. As far as writing something is concerned, the reader really doesn't exist. The writer's business is somehow to create in the work something which will stand on its own and make its own demands; and if the writer is good he discovers what those demands are, and he meets them, and creates this thing which readers can then do what they like with. Gertrude

Stein said, "I write for myself and strangers," and then eventually she said that she wrote only for herself. I think she should have taken one further step. You don't write for anybody. People who send you bills do that. People who want to sell you things so they can send you bills do that. People who want to tell you things so they can sell you things so they can send you bills do that. You are advancing an art—the art. That is what you are trying to do.

Interviewer: How important is it to you to establish some verisimilitude of character to release language?

Gass: Not terribly important. But what you are suggesting is. What I want to do is establish the legitimacy of the verbal source, which is sometimes a character, but it is sometimes a situation or some other kind of excuse. It must seem the right source. You mustn't turn on your tub tap and get crankcase oil. But this has little relationship to how people actually might talk of how oil might actually flow. People tell me that my characters are going crazy, and perhaps they believe that because I don't pay enough attention to verisimilitude. I don't think they are crazy, but the heightened language, the rapid shifts of feeling, the kinds of construction I am fond of—these do make readers think that the mind they are experiencing is not an ordinary one, that the consciousness they've been made conscious of is unusual, and that therefore it must be unhinged, extreme. I have a problem with dialogue because it is difficult for me to envision the total context in which the heightened language I sometimes want to use for conversation is justifiable.

Interviewer: It seems to me that a number of the voices in your fiction are obsessional.

Gass: That's an impression which may come from my methods of construction. A particular piece is likely to be the exploration of a symbol or a certain set of symbols, and this constrains the text. No meaning can go away without returning. If you're writing an ordinary naturalistic novel, you would be normally interested in the range and extent of experiences and responses and other people. I'm not. You'd want to give the impression of a large world, as if the land was larger than the feet of your fiction. Like Lowry, I want closure, suffocation, the sense that there is nowhere else to go. Also I think the voices tend to reinforce the impression because I often locate the work in a single consciousness. Solipsism is one of the risks of the letter 'L' If we were really listening in on any person's subconscious talk, it would sound pretty obsessional. One is consumed by one's self.

Interviewer: Is "Icicles" a kind of sport for you? It does create a voice—the real estate salesman—we might hear on TV.

Gass: The central images I wanted to develop led to that—basically the idea of the icicles as a kind of property, then as part of real estate. And pretty soon I was into the real estate business. I couldn't give this language to the main character, but I did want to carry a certain notion of property forward as far as possible. I sort of backed into that, starting—as I usually do—with a concrete symbol that I wanted to explore: what can I do with the image of the icicle. I ended up deep in philosophical materialism.

Interviewer: That is the way a lot of your stories start?

Gass: Almost. invariably now. The only story that didn't start that way was my first one, "The Pedersen Kid," which had its story line first. All the others have begun with a very concrete everyday image—insects, icicles—or in the case of the novel subordinate suns circling the larger theme of luck skipping stones, and so on. That's where the unity, if you can find it in my work, comes from. I am exposing a symbolic center. When I think the exposure is complete, I am finished with the story. It's more than peeling a peach.

I used to collect names as possibilities. Certain characters in a sense emerged from their names. I never conceive a character and then seek to christen it. I always have to have the words. I can't even get a story going until I have the title. The title, though, is a direct statement of the central image. If I try to think out in outline some linear structure, then I start pushing my material in that direction like a baby in a pram. When you arrive at your destination, all you still have is a baby in a pram. I want the work to write itself, every passage to emerge from the ones which have come before, so I have to keep looking at what I've done to see what will come out. Usually nothing does and I have to rewrite my beginning until something does suggest itself.

Interviewer: Do some of these images become emblematic for you? Spiders for example.

Gass: Yes, they become a certain kind of emblem. I am very fond of spiders. I am as fond of them as my family allows me to be. I used to have a house out in the country and it sheltered many spiders. Once quite a large handsome spider spun his web in the john where I could conveniently watch him. And of course the family wanted that ughyukky spider removed. I regarded it as a convenient symbol of the imagination: spinning, lying in wait, sucking dry. Maybe my family wanted the imagination removed. But partly I use the spider because, in general, I like insects. I like to watch them operate. I think animals have the same fascination, but except for a few household pets, you have to go out to the zoo to see them. You can watch a spider the way you can sometimes watch people on the New York subway. You can inspect them. Raccoons move too much, and are hard to get close to. That's one reason I spend a lot of time examining objects. They hold still. They aren't threatened or embarrassed by your stare. I don't *regard* as much as I once did, but I realized that I was looking for sources of language, and now my source of language is almost always other language instead of things in the world. Words are the supreme objects. They are *minded* things.

Interviewer: You described the most important intellectual experience of your life, seeing Wittgenstein, as almost wholly with content[sic]. How important is the notion of activity to you?

Gass: That was Wittgenstein's famous definition of philosophy: it was an activity, a certain way of doing which was without end. That notion is very similar to the one Valéry had about poetry. He was interested in the activity of writing, the consciousness in the act of composing, creating, and less so (he said) in the final result—which wasn't for him final, only the sign of an absolute weariness. Well, I'm very interested in the process of course. I can become my subject. But I am interested in the process because of what I want it to lead to—the story, the poem. Perfection. But the process is a great lure and you can postpone failure by dallying along the way like *Ulysses*. I can hardly get from one sentence to the next.

Interviewer: Is that why you write so slowly?

Gass: I write slowly because I write badly. I have to rewrite everything many many times just to achieve mediocrity. Time can give you a good critical perspective, and I often have to go slow so that I can look back on what sort of botch of things I made three months ago. Much of the stuff which I will finally publish, with all its flaws, as if it had been dashed off with a felt pen, will have begun eight or more years earlier, and worried and slowly chewed on and left for dead many times in the interim.

Interviewer: You've said that when you first started writing you wrote only sentences. Was this the result of your philosophical skepticism about language or a program of exercises?

Gass: Experiments. I have no skepticism about language. I know it can bamboozle, but I am a believer. No. My experiments were stimulated by my reading of Gertrude Stein. I didn't really get to know her work until I was in graduate school. Talk about having your head tipped. I suddenly realized that I don't know anything about the basic forms that I was supposed to be managing. Nothing. So I studied her very carefully. I am still studying her, and I have always learned a lot. She made me understand how little I knew about what could be done with the basic units of all writing. And she raised philosophical questions about what the basic unit really was, or whether there was one, and about the functions of grammar. In philosophy we were interested in some of the same things then, but we weren't then raising important esthetic issues. Now, every issue is esthetic. I don't know which is worse. But one of the wonderful things about Gertrude is that her repetitions rearrange the esthetic grammar of the sentence and impose this new or special grammar upon the ordinary syntax of English. When I started to examine what she was up to, I realized that I had to begin to get a feel, the way a painter would, of what happens when you try a sentence this way or try it that. To write sentences out of context is a fool's business, but I set about doing the fool's business. You can't really talk very sensibly about the content of a sentence out of the context of its use, but you can talk a lot about the form of the sentence and how the forms are interlaced and how they interact within a sentence. I practiced a long time, I mean a long time, writing sentences and connecting sentences and generally fiddling around. I think I learned something; But not enough. I'm still doing it.

Interviewer: How do you define the esthetic difference?

Gass: Much of it is musical, most of it is defined by the gut, and theoretically-well, it gets "defined" by negation. Most sentences are formed for the sake of communication. For efficiency, clarity; but rhetorical forms are there for the sake of effect, for persuasion. There are poetic forms too. Of course you end up simply feeling that things are going right or, alas, that they are not.

Interviewer: Does it have to go against the grain to be right for you?

Gass: I don't think so, but it's true that I'm unlikely to trust anything that isn't against the grain. I am unlikely to trust a sentence that comes easily. I should love to be able to write with ease, but I can't, and when I do push ahead or rush on, the result is invariably poor. I have a bad attitude toward things which come easy—wine, women, work, or song—an attitude quite false to the facts, of course.

Interviewer: Two words recur throughout your criticism—"model" and "metaphor." What is their importance to you?

Gass: I love metaphor the way some people love junk food. I think metaphorically, feel metaphorically, see metaphorically. And if anything in writing comes easily, comes unbidden, often unwanted, it is metaphor. *Like* follows *as* as night the day. Now most of these metaphors are bad and have to be thrown away. Who saves used Kleenex? I never have to say: "What shall I compare this to?" a summer's day? No. I have to beat the comparisons back into the holes they pour from. Some salt is savory. I live in a sea. But that's why I am so lost in the Elizabethans, because they seem to have sunk in the same ocean. What is not metaphorical, is not.

Leave nothing well enough alone is my motto, and I have been studying the phenomenon of language called metaphor since graduate school. Metaphor has been thought to be a pet of language, a peculiar relation between subject and predicate mainly: unhealthy, odd. But you can make metaphors by juxtaposing objects, and in lots of other ways. Suppose the relation between literary language and the world were itself metaphorical? Suppose the relation between language and life is like the relation between the subject and the predicate in a metaphor? If the analogy held, then one might find in it a way to express the relationship between literature and the world which wouldn't be quite so severe as the formalist position I once took required, and yet avoid the imbecility which makes it into some "meaningful" commentary. I've been principally interested in establishing the relationship between fiction and the world. If we can see that relation as a metaphorical one, then we are already several steps in the direction of models. Theory, in science; is frequently conceived as that which flows from a model. Indeed, making the model and constructing the theory are not always two different activities. The kinds of misinterpretation which arouse my wrath—not to say contempt—are paralleled, one finds, by misinterpretations of scientific facts-theories-laws which lead to paradoxes and confusions of every kind.

Interviewer: If fiction is a metaphor, what is a good metaphor for fiction?

Gass: I have thrown out a number of them and I wouldn't regard any of them as much good. A fiction is certainly not a mirror dawdling down a road. If I could think of a good one, I would put it in a novel. It's not an emotional model of the world—that's too narrow. It's more like a phenomenological model.

Interviewer: A character in *The Tunnel* is writing a limerical history of the world. Why don't you write poetry other than your limericks?

Gass: I can't. I would love to. When I was young I tried, but it was awful. Not just bad, but monumentally so. I tend to use the word "poetry" as a generic term for everything I approve of, but I am unable to manage those narrower forms for any length of time or with any success. I can explore prose sentences and prose paragraph structures. Those can be pretty tight sometimes, and certainly as formal as a poem. But when it comes to the damn poetry itself—well, I don't really know why I am so bad. Maybe I'm just a big dog and need a lot of room to turn around in. I can get away with a limerick because it is a very short form. I can turn out couplets, too, but not enough of them to make a whole poem. I have to be constantly discovering my form while I am working. In poetry, when you write the first two lines you have to have flung out the form fourteen or twenty-five lines ahead of you, but it takes me more than twenty-five lines to find the form I should have flung out ahead of me in the first place.

Interviewer: You mentioned "playing around with form" before. How does that work in, say, "In the Heart of the Heart of the Country"?

Gass: Suppose somebody says, "Why don't you write a piece of journalism about how it is to live in the Midwest?" It is not an interesting suggestion, and I don't think I am going to do it, but I nevertheless get curious. I take a few notes. I take a lot of notes. The notes are of themselves a kind of form. Here are a lot of little headings: under this, such and such, under that, so and so. Then you begin to see that you've got these little blocks of information, and you start thinking, maybe I could harden these up and move them around. So you start thinking what kind of pattern of presentation would achieve the best effect. It is like establishing a kind of very large sentence. You ask yourself what kind of existing form your notes are closest to. Notes! of course! you cry out. You can hear me, I imagine. And so word resemblance leads you on, not form. So you've really got a musical problem, certain paragraphs you are arranging, and you imagine you are orchestrating the *flow* of feelings from one thing to another. You want each note to have a certain integrity, but of course you are already thinking of how notes fit together. And you've got this private metaphor of notecard and note in music. Once you get your key signature, the theme inherent in the notes begins to emerge: the relationship between art and life and all that. And the town you've started to describe is called Brookston, but you don't want to call it that, and in a moment the B you've reduced it to is reminding you of Byzantium, which goes with the theme, so you decide to explore Byzantium poems, though

with an ironic twist. You start out with "So I have sailed the seas and come
. . . to B." Have I really come to be? No. Certain themes are developed that
parallel themes in Yeats. The story moves through a series of suggestions, of
formal relationships. And eventually what you want to do is take account of
the kind of formal relationship that begins to emerge simply from a set of
notes—simply from an accumulation of data—from the *flow of* commentary
and the appreciation of a set of poems. For me any piece is a play of various
forms against one another. When I am playing with forms, it is often simply
to find a form for something odd like the garbage. I love lists. They begin
with no form at all . . . often, anyway. A list of names is very challenging.
There is one right order and the problem is to find it.

Interviewer: You are doing this damn thing on the floor of your study,
shuffling and threading these cards—or forms. The reader is reading the story
once, ten times, twenty times. He will never catch up with you.

Gass: He doesn't need to. If you convey, in the kind of story I've been
going on about, if you convey a certain note-taking quality, a little crude
sociology, that's all that's necessary. All these other devices are primarily
for the psychological side of the creative process, not for the reader. The
reader has to feel a certain set of moves. He doesn't have to know the calcula-
tions. Still, if you took the trouble to label the sections of "In the Heart . . ."
as you would describe a rhyme scheme, you'd find a pattern. I played with
lots of different patterns before I found one that suited me. But what suits
ultimately is not the fact that something fits an abstract pattern. You have to
feel a resolution and a movement in the fit, otherwise it's no good. Most of
these formal tics are private.

Interviewer: Is much of the activity of your writing simply to amuse you
or interest you as an exploration with no hope that the reader will catch any
of this? Is it necessary for you in order to keep writing?

Gass: "Amuse" may be the wrong word because it hurts so much, but in
essence what you are suggesting is correct. Psychologically these games are
necessary. Every writer plays them, though what they are varies a good deal.
It is also a protective device which can be dangerous. You may feel that
certain things which you have put down on the page are justified because you
know how they satisfy your blessed apparatus. That, of course, won't do. I
think for most writers there are little private projects which each work under-
takes, and that these are best studied by people who are interested in the
psychology of the writer. The Homeric parallels in *Ulysses* are of marginal

importance to the reading of the work but fundamental to the writing of it. Proust had to be suckered by Bergson. And so on. These beliefs and these forms have to do with the security and insecurity of going forward into the void. Writers have certain compulsions, certain ordering habits, which are a part of the book only in the sense that they make its writing possible. This is a widespread phenomenon. Certain rituals have to be gone through, in cooking, for example, which don't affect the final product at all.

Interviewer: Sometimes a writer, Nabokov for example, will engross the reader in his little games. What then?

Gass: I'm in favor of fun. Nabokov surfaces a lot of his game, however, and forces the reader, or the assiduous commentator, into paper chases. I don't think much of that, though I guess the assiduous commentator gets no quarter. Nabokov wants people to follow his private games with the same kind of interest he takes in them himself. Sometimes the intricacies and the little secrets and the codes really work for the reader; things open up and then it is really quite wonderful. Powerful private symbols are related to this. Lowry, for example, was obsessed with certain things. All great writers are. Lowry put down those obsessions on the page and because they are there, he believes they will have an effect. It is the kind of error the beginning writer makes too—all this stuff that is so important to him never really gets to the page at all.

Interviewer: What is a working day like for you?

Gass: Well, we usually get breakfast and the kids off to school by 9 o'clock and I start to work soon after. It's essential that I be in the midst of something, so I try to quit work with new material that now needs revision in the typewriter. In the morning I can start right off working on those revisions and hope that by the end of the day, the process of revising will have sent me forward into some new material. If I get interrupted while I am, in a sense, at the end of something—a sentence, a paragraph, a scene—then I'm liable to have trouble getting back into things. At Yaddo I worked all morning, all afternoon, a great part of the evening, every day. At home I usually work in the morning and for a couple of hours in the afternoon. Lately I have been getting some work done in the evening, but that's because I have not been teaching at all. I haven't been talking about grading papers, preparing lectures, that sort of thing. The real writing process is simply sitting there and typing the same old lines over and over and over and over and sheet after sheet after sheet gets filled with the same shit. And then I discard or abandon material for weeks, months, during which time I start something new. Usually I have a great many projects going at the same time—in the sense that a start of some sort has been made. I get very tense working, so I often have to get up and wander around the house. It is very bad on my stomach. I have to be mad to be working well anyway, and then I am mad about the way things are going on the page in addition. My ulcer flourishes and I have to chew lots of pills. When my work is going well, I am usually sort of sick.

Interviewer: Did Jethro Furber take over *Omensetter's Luck* because of this methodology?

Gass: He certainly did. Furber went through a lot of midwives being born. When I first wrote the book, Furber wasn't even in it. That was the version that was stolen. Then I rewrote it to get the stolen version back. Furber was still not there. I looked at what my memory had regained from the thief and concluded that the book, although it was now much better than the original, was really no good. It was then that Furber began to emerge. The book began to be the book I should have been writing all along. Now a lot of people find that the Furber section is where the book goes to hell. As far as I am concerned, it is the only justification for that book.

Interviewer: Is Furber the hero of *Omensetter's Luck* because he has the best rhetoric?

Gass: Yes. In my books, if anybody gets to be the hero, he's got the best passages. Hamlet has the best lines. Milton's Satan has the best lines. Furber is what the book turned out eventually to be all about. That's not quite right. It's rhetoric the book is about, and *The Tunnel* is about rhetoric too. It's more completely, more single-mindedly about rhetoric, about the movement of language and the beauty and terror of great speech. Omensetter is certainly not the major figure because he is basically a person without language. He is a wall everybody bounces a ball off. Now anybody who emerges in my work with any strength at all is somebody who has a language and that's why he's there.

Interviewer: Do you like the stories still?

Gass: As soon as I finish something it's dead, so my writing a preface about it, as I've just done, is very hard. I rarely read things that are in print when I give a reading somewhere. I publish a piece in order to kill it, so that I won't have, to fool around with it any longer. The best I can say is that when I have to look back on the stories I am sometimes not too terribly ashamed. *Omensetter's* got more passages which make me blush. There is one story in the collection which still suits me in the sense that when writing it, I did fundamentally what I wanted to do. That's "Order of Insects." I think that's the best thing I ever wrote.

Interviewer: How have visual art and music influenced your practice of fiction?

Gass: The kind of aesthetic necessary to comprehend the modern movement in painting up through, let's say, abstract expressionism, is one which I find very congenial. In great part, it preceded the development of a similar kind of theory for literature. I think the impact of formalism, constructivism, and so on, was very great in the visual arts, even though music had been free to go its independent way for some time. Painting, though, had seemed to be about things, had seemed to be mimetic in a basic way, and now it was possible to see how such vulgarizations might be abandoned, and real purity achieved. There were great paintings which didn't get their artistic value from some sort of statement they were making about the world. Then we could begin to wonder whether it was Fra Angelico's piety or his genius as a painter that make his paintings so wonderful. For him, of course, piety and painting were one. Not for us, though. There's nothing new about non-representation, of course, but it is still very much misunderstood, and very much opposed.

Interviewer: There's a lot of theorizing now about silence. Are you ever tempted by silence?

Gass: Obviously not. No. I think I am perfectly aware of the dangers and limitations of language. But the people who are talking about language running out as if it were the oil supply, or of reaching beyond language, as if there were a better plate of peaches just beyond the pears—well, that's just cheap romanticism. Beckett likes to work with silences the way a musician works with rests, though he works within a linguistic context, and even if he lowers and restricts his vocabulary, it is all language, nevertheless, and language is all he is basically interested in. Then this glorious emptiness is employed as a romantic cliche by people who persist in using language all the same. They say they are going beyond the limits of language toward something or other and this excuses their execrable style. No matter. They will pass away.

The fact remains that we are moving away, in terms of science and other communications systems, from what one ordinarily calls language. I remain interested in what we are going to use to talk to ourselves with. One of the fundamental problems with film is not simply its easy effects, and its conceptual poverty. That may in time be overcome. Film may be able to carry universals in a useful way. But you can't show films to yourself. There is no way of communicating inside your head but speech. And if you can't talk well to yourself, who can you talk to? You simply aren't anybody. I frequently imagine people who get bored with their own talk, who don't talk to themselves very much. Talk is essential to the human spirit. It is the human spirit. Speech. Not silence. That's also Beckett's point.

Interviewer: Does the aggressive motive you mentioned earlier make you a crabby reviewer?

Gass: I've been crabby about a few books, but I'm not often very mean. In a way I regret the times I have been, because I am rarely angry with the author. Once in a while you run into work which is actually corrupt. But by and large, I get crabby with critics. What happens is that you don't write against the book, whatever it is, but against some asinine prevailing critical climate in which the book appears. All these writers who have been touted as great—it is not their fault that they are just poor writers like the rest of us, trying to do their best, and having the damn bad luck to be praised by fools because they write so badly fools think they understand them. And the clubhouse journalists, the critics, who fall first for traditional kitsch, then experimental kitsch, for the latest French fad, for obfuscation, sensationalism, who are eager to froth at the mouth with the latest rage, with a collection of biases as large as the unemployed, and no standards, no nose for quality . . . well, as you can tell, it makes me mad, and so sometimes I light on the book. Which isn't a bit fair to the author. I've sworn not to do that anymore. Then there are times when I bitch about a biographer because the biographer is not interested in precisely these qualities in the subject which caused, presumably, the biography to be written in the first place. Then there are other problems. How can you write well enough to write about Colette? find the verve required for Henry Miller, the depth for Lowry, or for Borges the proper philosophical wit?

Interviewer: Who are some living novelists you respect?

Gass: Well, the question leaves out so many dead ones who are more alive. I think Barth is one of the great writers. I have admired his work since I first encountered it. I think he is incredible. Several of his books, in particular *The Sot-Weed Factor,* are the works which stand to my generation as *Ulysses* did to its. His habits of work are wholly unlike mine, and the kind of thing which engages him is quite different too. He is a great narrator, one of the best who ever plied the pen, as they used to say. He has been accused of being cold, purely mental, but I find him full of passion and excitement. And what I like about his work in great part is the unifying squeeze which that great intellectual grasp of his gives to his work, and the combination of enormous knowledge with fine feeling and artistic pride and energy and total control. I really admire a master. He's one.

A lot of the work of Hawkes is extraordinary, breath-taking. Everybody likes Beckett. Now. It's silly to mention Bellow, Borges, Nabokov—so obvious. And of course Stanley Elkin's work I like enormously. Some of Coover's too, I find extraordinarily interesting. Control again. Gaddis. Control. Also Barthelme—a poet. A great many South American writers write rings around us. Infante's *Three Trapped Tigers is* a great book. I taught *Hopscotch* once. I'll never get over it. Marquez, Fuentes, Lima, Lhosa . . . It is always an exciting time to be a reader. Lots of European writers are overblown, especially some of the French experimentalists, but Italo Calvino is wonderful. Thomas Bernhard's *The Lime Works* is impressive. In general, I would think that presently prose writers are much in advance of the poets. In the old days, I read more poetry than prose, but now it is in prose where you find things being put together well, where there is great ambition, and equal talent. Poets have gotten so careless, it is a disgrace. You can't pick up a page. All the words slide off.

Interviewer: Have you ever read anything about your work that interested you?

Gass: It all interests me when I start to read it, but soon the critic is explaining to me what I meant, and then I get bored (whether I agree with what's being said or not). I start to skip. But even a good critic isn't likely to tell me anything about my work I don't already know, since I'm pretty careful and self-conscious in what I do. I also don't take much pleasure in approval. I have been well treated by critics on the whole. I would like to be deeply pleased by what they say, but my pleasure doesn't last very long. A two second rush of warmth to the head, that's all. I feel a certain sense of relief that I got away with it again—that the critic didn't dislike it. Once in a while a negative criticism will be perceptive. You protect yourself from critics, of course, by anticipating all their censures, so you can say, "Yes, of course, I saw that long ago."

Interviewer: If you were going to write an essay on your own work, what would you concentrate on?

Gass: I think I would immediately start talking about the manipulation of language, and I'd end writing just another essay on style. If I am anything as a writer, that is what I am: a stylist. I am not a writer of short stories or novels or essays or whatever. I am a writer, in general. I am interested in how one writes anything. So if I were to write about my own work, I would write about writing sentences.

Interviewer: Do you teach any creative writing courses?

Gass: I resent spending a lot of time on lousy stuff. If somebody is reading a bad paper in a seminar, it is nevertheless on Plato, and it is Plato we can talk about. Whereas, if somebody is writing about their hunting trip—well—where can one go for salvation or relief? Creative writing teachers, poor souls, must immerse themselves in slop and even take it seriously. Since I can't bear it, resent it, I shouldn't teach it. It is probably impossible to teach anyone to be a good writer. You can teach people how to read, possibly.

I am also aware of how little I can tolerate other people telling me how to write. So why should I do it to my students? I do not invite or accept this sort of personal criticism. I usually have poor to absent relations with editors because they have a habit of desiring changes and I resist changes. So why should I tell students to make changes? I also remember how bad I was. I wrote far worse stuff than I see from students. What can I fairly say to them?

Interviewer: You've said no decent sentence could come from a half-formed man.

Gass: I said that? I shouldn't have. Most writers are probably quarter formed. Hopeless and helpless. One's complete sentences are attempts, as often as not, to complete an incomplete self with words. If you were a fully realized person—whatever the hell that would be—you wouldn't fool around writing books.

An Interview with William Gass

Jay White / 1977

From *Colorado State Review,* New Series, 6.2 (Fall 1977), 3–12. Reprinted by permission.

Question: It seems as though on the one hand you are arguing against a literature that tries to be relevant to a social, political or moral framework, what Stevens called "the pressures of reality," but at the same time you've said in the *New Fiction* and elsewhere that you want the reader to actively participate in the work. How does the reader do that if he can't latch on to any sort of identifiable reality in the work?

Gass: I think it's something like this. This is very complicated. I think that we might distinguish between poetry and fiction in that what the fiction writer does is construct a metaphorical model of the world. Now, for a long time I thought fiction is really hermetically sealed off, and if you want any participation by the reader in the work, it's simply the total commitment that you would give, to say, Euclid. It's not you, the person, that's giving it, in the ordinary sense, it's your mind that is totally absorbed by the problems. But that didn't seem really quite appropriate to the way fiction has historically gone, and so my notion was that maybe fiction developed a metaphorical model of the world in which the reader was one side of the metaphor. The work of fiction would then be a work that stood as a metaphor for their existence. What happens is that the reader participates, actually lends himself to being a part of the work of art itself, by being the subject of the image. That was my idea. Now, I don't know if that will work. Just as you might say of something metaphorically, the rose, let's say, something really trite: the rose bled its petals. Now, there you are using metaphor as an image for the rose, but they are both in the linguistic situation, the word rose, the word petals, and so forth. But suppose a whole work of fiction like Beckett's *Endgame* was a metaphorical image of the audience. You would have one part of it, the performance (a verbal entity, *or* mostly verbal), and the other side of it would be in the world, the audience. Just as the reader might find himself as a part of the poem, or a part of a work as the subject. If that's the case, every book is about the reader, the way the phrase, bleeding rose, is about the rose.

Question: You are talking about a manipulation of forms that, in some sense, downgrades the content, so that the reader must penetrate into the significance of an autonomous construct, if he is to grasp the meaning and beauty of the work. Aren't you putting yourself into an elitist position when you ask the reader to grasp the form and not necessarily the content?

Gass: I don't think it's an elitist position. It's a position of aesthetic intention, a relationship to something else which it is, in a sense, structuring or informing. I think you can get a kind of continuum as you do in science to things which are largely fact-oriented in content, toward the very mathematical sciences which get very theoretical, and soon you are talking about ideal properties which have no direct, actual existence. I think that in literature, as in science, the value of a work rests parallel to the problem of validity, rather than to the problem of content. One of the ways of perceiving that is to empty the work of its content, the way a logician would, to see the relationships in form.

Question: But don't you still, somehow, want an interdependence between reality and how it is reshaped in the imagination? Otherwise, you have, let's say, Yeat's mechanical bird, but what sense does that convey, if there aren't real birds?

Gass: Well, the problem the way Borges would put it to us is: maybe the whole function of birds is to give us the mechanical bird which will replace the bird. Because what Borges is often talking about is creating a symbol: you start out with a sign for something and you think, well, the sign is dependent upon the thing, and it's just designating the thing, but there are lots of good reasons to suppose that the sign becomes more important and usurps the function of the thing, and even in a lot of our most important aspects of life, replaces it. What is fascinating is to see how the symbol suddenly assumes a greater reality than the thing it originally symbolized. You don't even need the object; it was a mere excuse for the symbol. That happens in religion all the time. Actually, it was a good thing you see with great religious leaders like Jesus. You want to pull them off the scene because their physical presence continues to be embarrassing. Suppose Jack Kennedy had stayed around and run a full term, then his too human qualities would have been before us all the time. If we want a deity, a symbol, we have to remove the reality that the symbol referred to, very quickly; else we will constantly be seeing that the symbol is falsifying the reality. It's the symbol that we want to embrace.

Question: That sounds a little like a revised Platonist position, in which language itself becomes on Idea, Concept, or Symbol, so that what the reader must do is perceive language as a container of consciousness, a way of seeing . . .

Gass: Of an increasingly independent reality.

Question: And that is the power of the work as you see it?

Gass: Yes, I think that works in fiction. Now, if you start talking about the world outside, philosophically, I have a lot of objections to it. I think it's a fictionalizing procedure; so, in effect, I'm a Platonist inside my aesthetic, that is, I want to treat language as a Platonist would treat forms, but I'm not a Platonist outside, philosophically.

Question: I'm still failing to see how the reader can interact with the work, what he has at stake in reading the work, if he can't relate to the significance of the Form, or the idea of Language as a container of consciousness?

Gass: Well, then he's going to read it for other reasons and there may not be much there to react to.

Question: Because you don't think one should be reading the work for any other reason than language as an aesthetic device for addressing an independent reality?

Gass: Oh, sure, you can read it for lots of other reasons. No, my complaint is not that, in fact, the more you can get out of a book, the better, in all different directions. But the question is whether or not you are going to judge it to be an aesthetically good book on the basis of this other stuff, that's all. I think what's important is that the judgement be directed toward the proper quality on the proper basis. People will call all kinds of books good, meaning artistically good. Now, if they just said good, in this other mode, fine. Take *Madame Bovary,* it's an indictment of society, a powerful social document with important social content. You couldn't read *Madame Bovary,* it seems to me, properly, and not see that, and respond to it. But if you are going to say that makes it artificially a great book, no, that has nothing to do with its artistic greatness. That's what I would say.

Question: At the same time, don't you think there might be some problems with just the manipulation of certain techniques without the author revealing the significance of these techniques? One of the things that characterizes a lot of contemporary poetry and fiction is its ability to be stylized and have a very striking veneer, containing a surreal, dazzling quality, but one often can't puzzle out the substance and life behind it. All the reader gets is technique.

Gass: Yes, there is a problem there, but the problem, however, is not one of form, but of technique, which is a different kind of animal. There are a great many painters, for example, who have great technique, which means they can carry out their intention, because they are able to do whatever they want, but what they want to do is trivial. We can see this carried out, perfectly, with Dali. He has great technique, but nothing but junk. What you want are forms which are sufficiently profound within the mode that they are infinitely explorable, and this both very easy and very hard, because the relationship between the number one and the number two is infinitely profound and difficult. The structure of certain pieces by Bach is infinitely explorable, yet there is nothing there but these relationships. Now, it means that those relationships have been profoundly explored, and not just superficially, and that's my complaint about a lot of writers who write "well." They have the technique and yet they don't write well at all because they have no penetration at all of the problem. We distinguish that way in philosophy all the time between component philosophical work, of which there is a good deal, and work that carries real profundity, real power.

Question: What new form are you trying to create in *The Tunnel* that's different from your earlier work? *In the Heart of the Heart of the Country*, and *Omensetter's Luck*?

Gass: In those works, the conception and the form sort of topsied. I just struggled along. The problem with *Omensetter* was that the form I tried to impose on it didn't quite jell. And so the problem for me was not to find a form I could put down on top of it, to make it go together, make it respectable, but a form I could elicit from the material, and that's like staring at a leaf until you see the structure of its growth. Now the problem here in *The Tunnel* is that you've got something growing, but you don't have any law of its growth, and you're trying to find that law so I have to keep going back to the material that I've got to see if I can find what form it has, and make that form more manifest, more pure, and then see if I can get a form that will generate the structure. That's one of the reasons why I've been so slow. I don't recommend it.

Question: So, the form of the work for you is discovered in the process of doing it, and not imposed from without, in terms of an artifice we could discuss in abstract considerations?

Gass: Right. Some people write like John Barth; he knows exactly where he is going. He has got it all laid out. I've forgotten the exact proportions he gave me but I said, "Well, how are you coming along on your book, Jack?" He said, "Oh, I'm about seven/elevenths done." I'd love to know where I was going; but he is not really imposing; it's very comfortable for him. For me, that's very uncomfortable, and I start falsifying the stuff and pushing it around to go something laid out in advance, and it never works. I always have to try and figure out from what I've done what should come next, and then I find out from looking at this lump that I can't see anything that comes next. If I can't see anything that comes next, I have to rewrite what I've done until there is something that comes next. So, I rewrite that, and when I rewrite that it becomes a bigger lump, and that's what comes next. I do that for ten years, and then maybe I've got a book done. It's a dumb way to write.

Question: You mentioned the Spanish, Mexican, and South American writers as being on the forefront of experimentation in regard to form. My understanding of them is that one of the reasons for their popularity is because they have the ability to enter into people's bloodstained lives, to speak to them through lived experience, particularly poets. Neruda, Vallejo and writers like Fuentes, Llosa and others.

Gass: That's why they are popular all right, but that's not why they are good. The ones particularly influenced by the surreal quality of Neruda and others in American poetry have at least concentrated on that—that is what has struck them most. But, of course, what I'm saying about formal properties would certainly only apply to the interests of certain poets in this country, and only a few novelists. I mean very minority report. Most novelists are still concerned with its content, with truth. I'm, only interested in a manipulation of language, as a writer that is but I think it is a minority position.

Question: Someone earlier today mentioned Gabriel García Márquez. To my way of thinking, there, much going on in terms of revolutionary form, not in his stories or in his major work *A Hundred Years of Solitude*. It seems to me, in a direct way, to be a straightforward narrative, with a few twists and cyclones.

Gass: Except the new book which I gather is very different. Yes, he is less technically spectacular.

Question: Do you appreciate him less for that?

Gass: No. What he does is marvelous. I mean he is just not the experimenter of other writers. A lot of people who aren't experimental achieve much more finished work, much more perfect. I don't see any reason for experimenting just for the hell of it, but I like experimental work and I'm interested in it. You know a lot of the experimental novels that come out are interesting, but are not valuable as total productions. There is some experimental work in Katherine Anne Porter's stories, but she is not fundamentally a wild experimenter. I would give anything to have written stories like that. I mean who cares as long as they are beautiful. I have to be an experimenter because I'm not that good. So, I've got to find other things, make my contribution somewhere else. But, of course, there are a lot of South American writers who are very experimental. Fuentes has written a great number of fairly conventional books, but the new one appears to be quite unconventional, and then most of the others are really quite extraordinary.

Question: You've mentioned in *The New Fiction* that you are particularly fond of Rilke. What is the special appeal in Rilke, and how is he instructive or important to your work?

Gass: There are a lot of different ways. I read Rilke very impurely, that is, I can respond to him on a number of different levels. One of them is an aesthetic that he develops which I think is very profound and important. And then, his way of seeing things, independent of the artistic view, strikes home very strongly with me. I have a kind of affinity for it, and so he moves me in that sense, very much, personally.

Question: But in some ways, he is a traditional poet dealing with deep, recognizable human themes, not formal aesthetic questions.

Gass: Oh sure, he thought he was bringing a new vision. If I want my theory to sound nice, I go read Valéry, then I feel theoretically much more comfortable. And I like Valéry, immensely, but Rilke, does something very, very deep and immediate for me, that only a few writers do.

Question: Do you mean, thematically?

Gass: No, it's almost psychological. It's not true of the themes he chooses, but some sort of way he writes, or the way he looks at things that hit me in a particularly, submerging way. Lowry does this to me; I feel swallowed up by Lowry. It's a terrifying experience to read him and it's terrifying to read Rilke.

Question: That surprises me because certainly there is no one more concerned with mapping out content, no one more autobiographical than Lowry, and even Rilke's life is really out front in his work, particularly in the *Elegies* where many of the operative symbols are taken from his childhood. How do you reconcile what is profoundly moving to you as a person, with what you are postulating in theory about the significance of form?

Gass: I just do what the phenomenologists call "bracketing." I've sometimes been accused of being some kind of freak for that, but I have very little difficulty in just bracketing certain considerations out. Now, I'm interested in Rilke as a person because he raises certain problems about the relationship of the writer to his material, theoretical issues about autobiographical stuff, and he's marvelous for the theory of inspiration. But in a theoretical way I am not interested in him as a person; whereas Colette I would crawl in bed with if I had the chance. But Rilke's particular way of working and seeing is distinctive.

Question: You mentioned inspiration and that topic indirectly ties in with this notion of technique. There's at least one point of tension between the Rilke/Proust school that claimed inspiration as a source behind their writing and someone like Nabakov, who said, "I distrust Proust, no one writes from inspiration." For him, there is only craft, only total control and manipulation, of what I see as largely complicated technique. I mean *Pale Fire* is little more than a massive job of cross-reference work and cross-wiring.

Gass: You know something about him. I've always had mixed feelings about Nabakov. Again, this technique problem. Recently, I've gotten interested in a composer that I've never liked much, Liszt. What suddenly struck me about Liszt was that he was the Nabakov of his day. He had this enormous technique and what he did was begin to make works not out of a sensibility, which was crude, but out of the technique itself. So I started listening to some of his pieces, not from the point of view of the Hungarian ghoulash that you sometimes find in it, some of the cheaper things, but in terms of transforming the whole problem of technique into a sensibility. And I think Nabakov, at his best, does that. What he is at his worst, it's self-indulgent fireworks from which you can learn a great deal, but it turns out to be just cardboard emptiness. The same thing happens to Liszt, at his worst; it's this great technique, enormous skill, great formal maneuvering, incredible things happening, and you still sit there knowing it is very bad. So, I think *Pale Fire,* for example, is really a powerful book, but it's powerful the way a Liszt sonata is powerful. The technique suddenly transforms, escapes, gets above it.

Mr. Gass's appearance was sponsored by the Colorado State University Fine Arts Series. Their assistance in obtaining this interview is greatly appreciated.

William Gass and John Gardner:
A Debate on Fiction

Thomas LeClair / 1978

From *The New Republic,* 10 March 1979, 25–33. Reprinted by permission.

This discussion between William Gass and John Gardner took place on October 24, 1978, during a Fiction Festival sponsored by the University of Cincinnati and the National Endowment for the Arts. The discussion was moderated by Thomas LeClair, who teaches at Cincinnati. John Gardner is the author of *On Moral Fiction* and many novels. William Gass, novelist and teacher of philosophy, is the author most recently of *The World Within the Word,* a volume of literary criticism.

Thomas LeClair: Is there a use of language in fiction which is inherently moral?

John Gardner: When I wrote *On Moral Fiction,* I was talking about a particular kind of fiction which I think is consciously moral, fiction which tries to understand important matters by means of the best tool human beings have. Many of the most academically popular writers of our time are completely uninterested in understanding these matters. They are more interested in understanding juxtapositions than in understanding how we should live. They are concerned with making beautiful or interesting or ornate or curious objects. As for language—when I talk to you, I speak English and try to choose words, from all the possible words in the world, which seem most likely to say what I mean. If I am writing and find that one of the words that I choose is wrong, I put in a better word for my precise meaning. While English is just noises that we make with our mouths, teeth, throat, lungs and so on, fiction is an enormously complicated language. It has much more discreet, much more delicate ways of communicating. When I create a character, I want to make a lifelike human being, a virtual human being. Maybe by using the right kind of weather [sic], I can give you a hint of what this person is. By comparing him to a bear or a rhinoceros or a spider, I can give you another hint. In other words, everything I choose in writing a piece of fiction is aimed at communication. I think that beauty in fiction is finally elegant communication, where the very form of the work helps to say what I'm trying to say. If I'm writing about an ordered universe, I write an ordered novel. If I'm talking about a tension between order and disorder, I write a novel in which the form expresses that tension. But always I'm using the tool of language to dig a hole. Other people sometimes use the tool of language to chew on.

William Gass: John's saying that a number of contemporary writers are really not interested in solving problems is a little misleading. I think the difference lies in whether they believe one can understand important human issues by writing novels; they might be so concerned with these problems that they would rather not trust the solution of them to novelists. My own feelings are, of course, that moral issues surround us everywhere, that they are deeply important, and that the survival of the human race is necessary so that parasites like myself can diddle away in corners. The question that lies between John and me here is whether or not writing fiction, rather than, for instance, doing philosophy, is a good method for such an exploration. Philosophy has its own disciplines, its own methods of coming to clarity about these issues, so the way one talks about them won't twist the conclusions. Because fiction is a method which, by its very nature and demands, deforms, I am suspicious of it. John goes on to say that in writing he faces the problem of revision and getting his best words by constantly asking "Is this really what I believe?" I think that's fine. I don't care how the right words get on the page as long as they're the right words. But my condition is much bleaker. I don't know, most of the time, what I believe. Indeed, as a fiction writer I find it convenient not to believe things. Not to disbelieve things either, just to move into a realm where everything is held in suspension. You hope that the amount of meaning that you can pack into the book will always be more than you are capable of consciously understanding. Otherwise, the book is likely to be as thin as you are. You have to trick your medium into doing far better than you, as a conscious and clearheaded person, might manage. So one of the problems that I face is exactly the opposite of John's. John's concern is to communicate; I have very little to communicate. I'm not sure I understand what little I do have. I think it would be thin and uninteresting and hardly useful. If I did want to communicate, I would move over to philosophy and submit to the rigors that are concerned with the production of clarity, of logical order, truth and so on. In fiction, I am interested in transforming language, in disarming the almost insistent communicability of language.

When you are not asserting, you are not confusing, and I would be happy to avoid that.

T.L.: Does this kind of purity of creation have a moral value in the world as well as an aesthetic one?

W.G.: Sure, John wants a message, some kind of communication to the world. I want to plant some object in the world. Now it happens to be made of signs, which may lead people to think, because it's made of signs, that it's pointing somewhere. But actually I've gone down the road and collected all sorts of highway signs made a piece of sculpture out of these things that says Chicago, 35,000 miles. What I hope, of course, is that people will come along, gather in front of the sculpture and take look at it—consequently, forgetting Chicago. I want to add something to the world which the world can then ponder the same way it ponders the world. Now, what kind of object? Old romantic that I am, I would like to add objects to the world worthy of love. I think that the things one love, most particularly in other people, are quite beyond anything they communicate or merely "mean." Planting those objects is a moral activity, I suppose. You certainly don't want to add objects to the world that everybody will detest: "Another slug made by Bill Gass." That's likely to be their attitude, but you don't hope for it. The next question is, why is it that one wants this thing loved? My particular aim is that it be loved because it is so beautiful in itself, something that exists simply to be experienced. So the beauty has to come first.

J.G.: There's no question that an object made simply to be beautiful is an affirmation of a kind, and any affirmation of that which is good for human beings is moral. But Bill and I, in our writing, are concerned with different kinds of affirmation. When I write, I try find out, by honest thought, moment by moment, psychological response by psychological response, what it is that I can affirm as true and good. I think, for example, it's better to be an American democratic person than a headhunter. I think I think that. When I work it in a novel, I might change my mind a little. But in the process of discovering what I really believe, what I can say yes to: "yes, I affirm that, that's good, that's helpful to people, that makes it possible for individuals to live in society," in the process I create an effect.

By telling a moving story, I've led the reader to an affirmation of the value I have come to find that I can affirm. The difference between what I am doing and what a philosopher is doing is that my activity leads to a feeling state, whereas the philosopher has only cold clarity. I'm after an affirmation of how to live, but it's a difficult affirmation. Again and again people read my books and misunderstand the endings; they think the end of *Grendel* is a curse. It's such a marginal affirmation that maybe it might as well be a curse. There isn't an awful lot one can affirm, but I try to get the affirmation that I can really believe and that will move people. I'm trying for an affirmation that has something to do with how to live; Bill and other writers like him are trying for an affirmation of just living. A guy walks along a street and sees this magnificent sculpture made out of signs and his day is better for it. But what I want the guy to do is continue past the signs and go do his job.

W.G.: One of the problems that I find with John's view is that it might lead you to say harsh things about great writers, a terrible thought. Suppose you have a writer who clearly inspects what he believes and ends his great long work by saying "You must go on, I can't go on, I'll go on." That's about as affirmative as Beckett gets, and there are other writers who, in following a process of being honest about what they can affirm, find only "going on" left and are not even sure of that without writing another book to make sure they're still going on. Gaddis hasn't made a habit of hooray. Since I think, quite independently of any theory that Beckett is one of the greatest writers of this period, I'm wondering, John, if your view allows you to regard him in that way?

J.G.: I don't think that's a problem because one is terribly moved by Beckett and one does go on, and one even feels he has a reason for going on, although the reason may be in the technical sense absurd. There are other writers who would persuade you not to go on, that everything is nonsense, that you should kill yourself. They, of course, go on to write another book while you have killed yourself. If we look back through the history of litera-ture, those writers have not been the ones who have been loved and who have survived. Again and again we're moved by Achilles, we're moved by the best of Shakespeare, Chaucer and others we keep going back to. Writers who give us visions to which we say, with all our unconscious minds as well as our conscious minds, "That's just not so," we don't read.

I'm not saying that other people shouldn't make wonderful sculptures; I am saying they shouldn't be mistaken for the big tent, the most important kind of work. The theory that I'm proposing says, fundamentally, that you create in the reader's mind a vivid and continuous dream. The reader sits down with his book just after breakfast, and immediately someone says, "Hermione, aren't you coming to lunch?" One instant has passed although

200 pages have passed because the reader has been in a vivid and continuous dream, living a virtual life, making moral judgments in a virtual state.

. . . The real problem with this argument is that Bill Gass is a sneaky moralist. His book ends in magnificent affirmation. I'm arguing against his theory, but his books don't follow it.

T.L.: Bill, what about this vivid and continuous dream?

W.G.: It's rather imaginary. In music, let's say, the motion of the work comes from the performance. That's true also in the theater. So if there's an interruption, or your mind goes blank or someone rattles a bag, you miss something and that's too bad, it's lost. In reading fiction, however, the motion that moves the text comes from the reader. Now the writer can indicate or try to indicate how that motion should go and at what rate. But I don't think that anyone writes a book now supposing that the reader will sit down and read 200 pages through in a dream. He's going to, in fact, stop, brush a fly off his nose, go back to the first page, read it over, skip, look around for the juicy parts. The book is more like a building which you're trying to get someone to go through the way you want them to. The experience of a novel can occasionally be what John describes. I remember it happening when I was 12 or so reading *Boy Scout Boys on the Columbia River.*

J.G.: You're right if you're talking about the concert hall, but with a record you can go back. And when you go back, you remember what came before, you know where you are, and you know where you're going. If a novel is plotted, if you have the actualization of the potential that exists, in a character in a certain situation, then the argument of the novel—the movement of the plot, the development of the characters in their response to problems—leads you through the novel. What argument is to philosophy, plot is to fiction. Most philosophers set up a syllogism and move steadily through it. You have a feeling of profluence, of forward flowingness. When a novel has a plot, it doesn't matter if the reader goes to chapter eight, then ducks back to chapter five, and then goes forward again. Finally, the ultimate apparition, the ultimate dream of the novel, is a continuous one. When you decide as a writer that the novel is just a house you're trying to get somebody to go through in various ways, you have broken faith with the reader because you are now a manipulator, as opposed to an empathizer. If the novelist follows his plot, which is the characters and the action, if he honestly and continuously proceeds from here to here because he wants to understand some particular question, the reader is going to go with him because he wants to know the same answers. On the other hand, if the writer makes the reader do things, then I think he puts the reader in a subservient position which I don't like.

Let me elaborate with the plot of a story someone told me once. A woman has had a perfect marriage. After her husband dies, she finds a walnut box of perfectly labeled feathers in the garage. She finds out that all his life he has had a secret hobby, and at that moment she begins to wonder how come he didn't tell her? The next time she hears a conversation about her husband, she's going to listen in a different way. The next time her kids talk about him, she's going to listen in a different way. The next time she meets his 30-year-old secretary, she'll look at her a different way. We're on to a real problem, which is human doubt, human faith, and as long as we're on that, we don't want the author pushing us around. We want someone honestly, gently taking us through an exploration of this situation. There is an act of faith, whereas when the author manipulates the reader he is solipsistic in the worst sense: he's not in a love relationship with the reader.

W.G.: I didn't mean the manipulation of the reader when I compared reading to going through a building. The kind of response to novels that John is talking about certainly was appropriate 200 years ago, when there were lots of novels written in that form. There are just not many of them being written that way anymore. When Fielding comes to the end of *Tom Jones,* for example, I suspect that he expects us to remember about as much of the first chapter as we would of that early part of our life, if we were thinking back. Not every detail, not every adjective attached to a noun in a certain way. In someone like Joyce, quite the contrary is true. He wants an experience that can happen only when the reader moves constantly about the book. The notion of the space in which this kind of book is constructed is quite different from the notion of the time through which the Fielding work moves. While I don't mind Fielding's having written the way he wrote, John begrudges some people writing in this newer or different way, in which the kind of attention the reader is expected to pay to the page transforms the way the work exists.

J.G.: I think we both agree that we're trying to create something that the reader will love. Is it possibly the case that the fiction you're advocating, Bill, is simply not lovable, that it simply doesn't hook readers? You can quickly Say, "But the most sophisticated reader. . . ." I'm not sure that's true. In the academy we teach Pynchon instead of Trollope. About Trollope there's nothing to say because it's all clear. On the other hand, every line of Pynchon you can explain because nothing is clear. So the academy ends up accidentally selecting books the student may need help with. They may be a couple of the greatest books in all history and 20 of the worst, but there's something to say about them. You get an artificial taste in the academy. The sophisticated reader may not remember how to read; he may not understand why it's nice that Jack in the Beanstalk steals those things from the giant.

W.G.: I suspect, John, that you want not things that will be loved but things that will be promiscuous. If you had a daughter to send into the world, would you want everybody to love her? I might be at my winery turning out bottles of thunderbird which everybody loves. It wouldn't give me much satisfaction. It's not just that books are loved, but why they're loved. If you've given them the properties that make them worthwhile, then it doesn't matter if no one does love them. Frequently very few people do or a work will go unobserved for years.

T.L.: Do the two of you write from different motives? We've heard love mentioned several times. I know that Bill Gass has used the word anger. Do the motives for your writing produce the differences in the kind of fiction that you write?

W.G.: I have a view I'm sure John wouldn't agree with. Very frequently the writer's aim is to take apart the world where you have very little control, and replace it with language over which you can have some control. Destroy and then repair. I once wrote a passage in which I had the narrator say "I want to rise so high that when I shit I won't miss anybody." But there are many motives for writing. Writing a book is such a complicated, long-term, difficult process that all of the possible motives that can funnel in will, and a great many of those motives will be base. If you can transform your particular baseness into something beautiful, that's about the best you can make of your own obnoxious nature.

J.G.: I agree with almost everything Bill says except the nonsense about human nature. I think human beings are a little lower than angels and a hell of a lot more important. One does take the world apart and put it back together, but I would express it differently. You write the book to understand and get control of in yourself things that you haven't been able to control and understand in the world. When you have the kind of problem that will come to you in repeated dreams, you work it out on the page. Maybe it's an illusory understanding, but I think it helps you live. I think with each book you write you become a better person. It's certainly true that a great many famous writers, Marcel Proust for instance, were awful human beings, were much better in their writing. The reason is, I think, that when one is writing a book

one gets to think over a nasty crack, and to gentle it and put it in a way that's
not quite so cutting. Bill might say it's more elegantly expressed. "I want to
rise so high that when I shit I won't miss anybody" is so well said the meanness is partly muted. It becomes a joke, a kind of self-mocking, so it's not
saying the same things that the writer might say if drunk and angry. I believe
that we revise our lives in our work and with each revision we find a mistake
we don't have to make again. I also think people become gradually slightly
better people as they write books. That may not be true, but that's my conviction.

W.G.: Do you think Alexander Pope got better as a person?

J.G.: I think that Bill values a great deal of literature that I don't value.
Alexander Pope expresses a mood that we all have—meanness—and he expresses it very well. But one ultimately says, "I don't feel like reading Pope
tonight. *Kojak* is on; I'll get my meanness quick." One always reads through
the mean writers with a certain amount of fascination, the same way you
watch the female praying mantis eat the male. But that doesn't mean you go
home every day and watch the praying mantises.

W.G.: Some of us do.

T.L.: The concept of character in fiction is one you differ on. Would you
talk about your notion of character?

W.G.: It's complex. I'll try to simplify it very quickly. A character for me
is any linguistic location of a book toward which a great part of the rest of
the text stands as a modifier. Just as the subject of a sentence say, is modified
by the predicate, so frequently some character, Emma Bovary for instance,
is regarded as a central character in the book because a lot of the language
basically and ultimately goes back to modify, be about, Emma Bovary. Now
the ideal book would have only one character; it would be like an absolute,
idealist system. What we do have are subordinate locales of linguistic energy—other characters—which the words in a book flow toward and come
out of. A white whale is a character; mountains in *Under the Volcano* are
characters. Ideas can become characters. Some of the most famous characters
in the history of fiction are in that great novel called philosophy. There's free
will and determinism. There's substance and accident. They have been characters in the history of philosophy from the beginning, and I find them fascinating. Substance is more interesting than most of my friends.

Now why would one adopt such awkward language—why not just talk
about character in the traditional sense? The advantage is that you avoid the

tendency as a reader to psychologize and fill the work with things that aren't
there. The work is filled with only one thing—words and how they work and
how they connect. That, of course, includes the meanings, the sounds, and
all the rest. When people ask "How are you building character?" they sometimes think you're going around peering at people to decide how you're
going to render something. That isn't a literary activity. It may be interesting,
but the literary activity is constructing a linguistic source on the page.

J.G.: I obviously don't agree with Bill on all that. It seems to me a character is an apparition in the writer's mind, a very clear apparition based on an
imaginative reconstruction or melting of many people the writer has known.
The ideal book has to have more than one character, because we know a
character by what he does: what he does to other people, and what they do
back to him. Bill wants to avoid the reader's "filling in," but when we read
J. D. Salinger, for instance, we understand many things about his characters
that aren't in the book because we know what people mean when they make
the gestures that Salinger's made-up people make. So we're all the time
seeing more of the picture than is given. In the good novel, the reader gets an
apparition, a dream, in which he sees people doing things to each other,
hurting each other or exploring each other, or loving each other or whatever,
and a tiny linguistic signal sets off a huge trap of material which gives us a
very subtle sense of these imaginary people. It's true that one can analyze
them as words on a page, but I have never cried at the fate of free will or
determinism in a good philosophy book.

Bill has argued that it's wrong to be frightened by a character in a book or
to cry at the death of a character. I say it's not. I say a book is nothing but a
written symbol of a dream. If someone jumps at me with an axe in a night-
mare, I scream and I have every right to scream because I believe that person
is real. In the same way, when the dream is transported to me by words and
I see that character leap out at me with an axe, I have every right to believe
that my head is going to be knocked in. I think it's very useful to talk about
character in the traditional ways. Contemporary philosophy has reconstructed
the world into its own words while distrusting the words that we've used over
and over and over. Meaning exists in literature because of the way thousands
of generations of people have used words. With just the slightest tap, you
ring the whole gong of meaning. I'm more interested in the gong than the
tap. I think Bill concentrates on the technique of the tap.

. . . First it matters to him that a novel is elegant and well-done and that it
has other characteristics I think are perhaps secondary. But given two well

done books, one of which strikes him as absolutely truthful while the other is not what he would affirm in his life, Bill would take, he says, the one that he thinks is true.

W.G.: Yes, but that's just wanting thickness to experience. If, for instance, I play golf for my health and to persuade some client and because I'm hooked on the symbolism of getting a ball into a hole, that's better than playing golf just to have a good score. But ultimately, whether you play golf well or not is determined by how well you score your performance—and that's what ought to be used as the aesthetic measure. If a beautiful book is a source of virtue and a source of truth—fine. That's jolly. The composer of such a work would be a fine philosopher or a noble saint, and an artist. But he's not a good artist because he's a fine philosopher or a noble saint.

. . . There is a fundamental divergence about what literature is. I don't want to subordinate beauty to truth and goodness. John and others have values which they think more important. Beauty, after all, is not very vital for people. I think it is very important, in the cleanliness of the mind, to know why a particular thing is good. A lot of people judge, to use a crude example, the dinner good because of the amount of calories it has. Well, that is important if you don't want to gain weight, but what has that got to do with the quality of the food? Moral judgments on art constantly confuse the quality of the food. I would also claim that my view is more catholic. It will allow in as good writers more than this other view will; John lets hardly anybody in the door.

J.G.: I love Bill's writing, and I honestly think that Bill is the only writer in America that I would let in the door. For 24 years I have been screaming at him, sometimes literally screaming at him, saying "Bill, you are wasting the greatest genius ever written to America by fiddling around when you could be doing big, important things." What he can do with language is magnificent, but then he turns it against itself. Our definitions of beauty are different. I think language exists to make a beautiful and powerful apparition. He thinks you can make pretty colored walls with it. That's unfair. But what I think is beautiful, he would think is not yet sufficiently ornate. The difference is that my 707 will fly and his is too encrusted with gold to get off the ground.

W.G.: There is always that danger. But what I really want is to have it sit there solid as a rock and have everybody think it is flying.

J.G.: Bill Gass is quoted as saying that his ambition in life is to write a book so good that nobody will publish it. My ambition in life is to outlive Bill Gass and change all of his books.

An Interview with William Gass

G. A. M. Janssens / 1979

From *Dutch Quarterly Review,* 9.4 (1979). Reprinted by permission.

William Gass was appointed to a distinguished professorship at Washington University, St. Louis, on 1 June 1979, the day this interview was conducted. He had just returned to St. Louis from New York City where he had received the Award of Merit for the Novel from the National Academy and Institute of Arts and Letters. Shortly before, *The First Winter of My Married Life,* a section from his novel in progress, *The Tunnel,* had been brought out in a limited edition by the Lord John Press.

G. A. M. Janssens: The modern interview takes many shapes. Nabokov made it almost into an essay form, polishing and rewriting. Do you see any virtue in the off-the-cuff character of the interview?

William Gass: I think there may be. What is interesting, almost more interesting than the words written down, is the preserved tapes; that is, I would like to hear interviews with Henry James because I would like to hear Henry James composing those elaborate sentences. The tone of voice more than any answers one might get. That can be done just as well by writing, and a great many interviews are polished and they are no longer off-the-cuff. I mean, Nabokov did not allow himself to be off the cuff. I don't like to correct too much in an interview because then it ceases to be an interview. One can tell, of course, reading the *Paris Review* interviews, which ones are really all written. But to hear the voice and the exchange would be for me very interesting.

Janssens: Have you written all your life; have you felt yourself to be a writer from a very early age, or was it a later discovery?

Gass: It is odd because there was no literary background in my family at all. My parents were both educated in an ordinary sense; my father was a teacher of mechanical drawing in high school. I was not precocious in any sense, and it would be hard to say exactly what year I wanted to be a writer, but 8 or 9 or whatever, and it is hard to even know what that meant to somebody that age and why. Certainly by the time I was in junior high school it was absolutely settled in my mind to be a writer. It was not clear exactly what, except that prose was fairly obviously the thing I wanted to do, even though I would have liked to have been a poet. I wrote all the way through highschool, journalism and so on, had a column, and wrote enormously, enormous amounts of stuff. It flowed out easily. I liked everything I wrote in those good old days.

Janssens: You were an undergraduate at Kenyon College, and then one thinks of the heyday of John Crowe Ransom, the early *Kenyon Review* and the New Criticism; but I gather all that has not been a great influence?

Gass: I went there in ignorance of the fact that it was such a centre. As a matter of fact, I didn't take any course in English when I was at Kenyon, when I was there in the first year; and the war interrupted and I came back, but I didn't take any courses in English. I sat in on Ransom's classes but I never took anything from him. I missed Lowell when he was there; that is, I saw him at a distance, but we never overlapped really. I never met Robert Frost when he was in residence. My college career was only two years really at Kenyon; the other part was just a mess—navy, junk—and I found quickly that I didn't take English classes well; I fought the professor, I was too smart to be taught, I thought I knew it all. I took some English courses later in graduate school—also had a little bit at Ohio Wesleyan when I was in the Navy, but mostly in graduate school at Cornell.

Janssens: Was Nabokov there while you were there?

Gass: Yes, and I was stupid enough not to go and find out what was going on in his courses. I knew he was—not a great writer, I didn't know that—I knew he was well-known as a campus curiosity. And then I started to read Nabokov just about the time I left. I had not read him before, but as soon as I started to read him I was of course absolutely knocked over. So I only met him once, didn't really know him at all. If I had started to read him sooner, I would have camped in his classes. I was quick to see that he was an incredible writer. It is part, I think, of his own American experience: people at Cornell didn't know how good he was and he was very bitter about it, understandably.

Janssens: This week's *New York Times Book Review* asks the usual question, you know: which hundred books do you recommend, etc., and they asked you, so let me quote you back at you: "Vladimir Nabokov's *Pale Fire,* his most perverse and brilliant book, yet not like *Lolita* which is cute." Could you clarify, that a little bit?

Gass: I think the problem I find with Nabokov's work is that at certain points his own great skills and his desire just to do tricks overcome him, and he plays with the reader. You feel sort of like a cat that has been forced to chase a rubber ball, as if . . . well, you are too tired, you don't want to do this, but, you know, you tease the cat and the cat has to respond. I have always found that about his work as the major flaw in it, but there are moments too, I think, when it doesn't hinder it; for one, when he is really deep into a kind of nostalgia trip. There his technical skills and his sardonic and ironic view of his whole art protect him from sentimentality—in a book like *The Defense* or in *Speak, Memory,* beautiful works in which he is really open to the emotion and he does not come around and say: Ha, Ha, I caught you crying in this passage, you dumb so and so. In *Pale Fire,* the opposite, where the technique, the problems of the craft become the object of his skill, and he has found a way to put that attitude to work within the work. But I think in *Lolita,* though there are many, many marvelous things in it, he leads the reader on a kind of paper chase; he plants some clues, he teases and so forth, and I keep falling out of the book watching him do these things too often. I think with someone like Nabokov you have the same problem as, say, with another incredible technician, Donald Barthelme. Especially when you have Nabokov's incredible skills, he has constantly to think up ways to push himself; otherwise what is the point?—and one can understand that.

Janssens: Yes, he does set himself these problems that he may or may not be able to resolve, and in the resolution is the pleasure. To what extent is that true of your own work also?

Gass: I have to set myself artificial problems or hazards in order to give myself shape, to shape the work. After a certain point, if the thing is going well, then it becomes the real problem and it is not a series of artificial barriers set up in advance. But at the beginning there usually is a hurdle. The idea, I think, is to get around that somehow so it's digested and disappears. My tendency is to create little problems, not so much in large, because I cannot see the whole so very easily in the work I'm doing, but let's say just in the paragraph. As the paragraph begins to develop, and I am having trouble with it, my resolution of that is to see the possibility of a certain shape to it and then impose very artificial conceptions upon it to give it form; and then you hope you can make it seem as if that's the way it should have gone. Otherwise it sprawls. And that technical interest surfaces, say, in a story like "The Pedersen Kid." When people say: what were you thinking about when you were writing that? I say: well, I have this technical problem of the alternation of long and short sentences and a limited vocabulary, and then they say, but what about the story? Well, you know, it is not up there in consciousness, it was all technical problems. When I am writing it is almost invariably a series of technical problems that immediately face you.

Janssens: You said recently, that the medium makes discoveries for you. I think that is a notion one finds in a number of contemporary authors whom one would not readily associate with you. I am thinking, for instance, of Philip Roth who turned his back on the tyranny of ideas in the sixties and said that he only really knew things after he had "sent them down through the blades of the fiction-making machine," as he puts it. Or Norman Mailer who writes journalism, but keeps talking about the big novel. Or Saul Bellow's irritation with the knowingness of the contemporary world and the "noise" of ideas. All these writers think of fiction as a more delicate instrument to explore reality than any other mode. Now you can of course say: I tackle certain problems, ideas, as a philosopher, but your notion that "you have to trick your medium into doing far better than you" intrigues me. I have a sense, though, that you mean something different from the other writers I mentioned.

Gass: I do, I think. For me the only thing that the writer can discover is things about the art itself. If I discover anything at all, which I generally doubt, it would be something about the art, and the aim of writing for me is to advance the art of writing, and that is what, for example, it seems to me, Nabokov is all about, what Beckett is all about, too. The themes, the obsessions that writers have, are absolutely essential to the long process of writing novels. It is such a long-term job, it involves such an enormous commitment of energy, that the whole person has to be bound up with it, so that there's got to be all kinds of personal idiosyncratic motives. These, however, don't really supply the fuel; they don't make the books good or interesting or anything else. What you indeed discover in reading a book, I think, is basically what the art is, what the art can do about itself. Now I find my students constantly telling me that by reading such and such a book they learn something they had not known before. I am always amazed by this, as if they had not paid any attention to existence. But for myself, I have both more, I think, and less skepticism about ideas than most writers. I guess one can say that Roth's present skepticism about ideas is due to the fact that he was not skeptical enough at the beginning. I was always skeptical of ideas in that sense, and as a philosopher, as a person who teaches philosophy, I am comparatively skeptic that you'd find a lot of truth in philosophy.

Janssens: Why did you differentiate just now between philosopher and teacher of philosophy?

Gass: Oh well, I am not a philosopher at all; I just teach philosophy. I have this feeling about all the arts: unless you are among the best you are nothing. Second is last in this business, and that is particularly true of philosophers. Second-rate philosophers are dreary, really dreary beyond belief, and how many great philosophers are there? You get six or seven in a century, you call it the Age of the Enlightenment. I have always felt that philosophy departments were pretentious beyond bearing, because they kept talking about turning out philosophers. It is like having a school of painting who believe that they are turning out artists: they are turning out people who paint; so what we in philosophy do is turn out people who teach philosophy. I met a philosopher once, Wittgenstein, and I know what a philosopher is. I have a distrust—not so much from Wittgenstein as a natural bent of mind—a very Wittgensteinian distrust of philosophical pronouncements, the difficulty of getting anywhere in the subject, so that that suspicion about ideas is very great. But the notion that literature was going to give them to me I never really had. For example, Rilke, I suppose my favourite writer really, and in the best sense a profound writer, is full of shit. I mean his ideas as nonsensical. As philosophical notions I have no respect for them at all, but as poetic notions they are absolutely beautiful. This is one of the reasons I am really a Heidegger hater, because Heidegger gets most of his ideas from Rilke and does not have the sense to see that this is great poetry. He projects it into religion, and I have an immense distrust of just that.

Janssens: I suppose that all fits in with the literary quarrel you and some others have been carrying on, for some time now with the literary establishment; a quarrel which people sometimes sum up rather sketchily by saying that you object to the linearity of traditional fiction.

Gass: I don't object to it on critical grounds in the sense that I find the linear novel perfectly acceptable. In other words, I am not saying there is something wrong with this; not at all. It is one way of organizing material, and it is natural to aspects of the material, to the medium itself at a certain level, and, therefore, one would normally suppose that the lean towards linearity in prose would be a very justifiable one. I think that the linear element in fiction is inescapable and must be dealt with, used just as it is in music, but there are other elements too, equally important. So I have a kind of view of a work as being layered: certain layers, or certain aspects of it, are non-linear and certain aspects are linear. Then what becomes interesting is the tension, the contrasts, contradictions between the layers, and I think it is true of many of the writers I admire that they are in a sense said to be breaking down—spatializing and breaking down—the linear, and that in many ways is true, but they are pointing to something. Barth, for example is probably as great a sheer narrator as there has been.

Janssens: That's interesting, because he seems to make a virtue out of linearity.

Gass: Yes, he is playing with that very notion. He is doing two things. His forms are spatial, incredibly spatial organizations. Even the notion, of course, of the frame-tale, whether it is the *Decameron* or the *Thousand and One Night* or whatever, is a spatial, inclusion thing. So what Barth is seeing is that a sentence even is in fact a linear process of enclosure—phrases, clauses, meanings enclosed inside of others, and logicians have always thought of logical processes in extensional terms, in spatial terms. So that what you have in Barth, I think, is this masterful narrator who is seeing, however, that narration is fundamentally conceptualized in spatial terms; so you have this beautiful tension which he sets up in things like "The Menelaid," or in the stories in *Chimera*. And it looks to me that *Letters* (Barth's new novel) is another where you are starting out with a form that is not only linear in just an ordinary sense but linear in temporal correspondence. It is obvious: letters are dated and are sent in temporal order and you have all of that, and of course what he is going to do with that obviously is dissolve it into an architecture. So both are very present. I think that the notion that contemporary fiction is anti-linear is too simple. Hawkes, for instance, has always worked in terms of linear forms, and in traditional ones like the detective story. What I mean is that the linearity is not just allowed to be a kind of naively accepted straightforward thing. My interest is to do similar kinds of things with what is a parallel, the essay, because I don't think I have anything new to contribute to the spatial organizations and rearrangements much in fiction; enormous things have been done and we are sort of digesting it all. But in the essay, you see, the expository development is a parallel to the narrative development, and I am very interested in seeing what can be done with that.

Janssens: Do you see strict lines of division between the genres?

Gass: No. I think that the genres are mixed up again, broken down, interpenetrated, but of course you have to have the genres in order to play that game. What is interesting, I think, is the increasing perception that the genre forms originally may have developed for certain very sensible purposes. To take a simple example: a railroad time-table; the very tabular way in which it is put down on paper reflects the kind of thing it is. Well, then pretty soon you begin to wonder to what degree the formal property is merely an expression of this need for communicating certain kinds of data and to what degree that formal property is changing the data. And then you start inventing time-tables, and fictionalizing, and when you start doing this you begin to play with the very notion of what form does, what structures are all about, and can you lift them out and move them around. I think in doing that, again it is too simple to say you are attacking the form. Let's suppose you start using a railroad timetable as a fictionalized form. You are not saying: time-tables is no way to list times for trains. It is a splendid way. Again, I think it is a failure of a sense of what is going on in people like the new journalists, because what they are really saying is: journalism would be better off if we mixed a little fictional techniques in with it. Now that is not true at all. It is worse off. Journalism is corrupted by that; but the sense of being able to take the forms and devices and move them around, to play with them without then supposing that you are improving on journalism, that's different altogether. I think you don't improve on history by incorporating a lot of fictional techniques; you just make history sloppy, careless . . .

Janssens: What about Robert Coover? In *The Public Burning* he takes, as a sort of nonfiction novelist, a historical event and fictionalizes it, but what comes out is, I think, very different from, say, Truman Capote's *In Cold Blood.*

Gass: Coover is really concerned to transform the reality of the event. Here you have the Rosenberg case which is so dismaying in its reality, so it provides an immediate challenge. It is a challenge to the art to take a journalistic event and treat it in terms of the jargon of the time, all the cliches, all the monkey business, transform it into an event in the book which will then manage to digest this into the work of art. Whereas with somebody like Truman Capote you are just using artistic tricks, fictional devices to jazz up and make your account more journalistically exciting, chilling, and so forth; perfectly standard devices and certainly not reprehensible, but it is not, I think, a desire to transform those events into art, and I think Mailer does the same thing. It is a very daring and huge—it is not a risk; I hate the word risk—but it is an artistic challenge to do what Coover was after in that book, particularly when you are working with striking public affairs about which of course the artist feels very strongly.

Janssens: Would you hold with John Barth who argues: o.k., you have the genre of the novel as a recognizable form, a document, and you can devise means of making it more real by being more precise in your description of the world around you. But you can also say: as a genre the novel is artificial and let's make the most of the very artificiality of the genre; you are then exploiting the unique features of the genre, rather than introducing elements from the outside in an effort to make fiction more real than it can ever be.

Gass: Yes, I think there is a competition, and an interesting one, in any book. There is the reality of the external world which the book may be in a sense pointing to, making references to, or pretending to make reference to, and the reality of the book itself; and·the best books, I think, always supplant and are more real. The problem is—and I think that is one of the things that Borges teaches, if literature teaches anything—that in many respects symbols are more real than the things they signify, and that what a novelist does when he is successful, is he invests his own work with a reality that is its own, and which it need not then constantly be borrowing from. It is like being born from parents: you come by resources in something which go on to be something yourself, and I think, again, art in general tends to take off from the world, but ends up by being a thing in itself, which then becomes part of the world again.

Janssens: What is your definition of the ideal reader?

Gass: He is somebody trained. Let's say the reader of Nabokov has to be the kind of person who immediately grasps without labour the kind of things Nabokov's art has put into it so that it comes out immediately. Then you don't get these questions about: "gee, wasn't it very complex the way he did all these things?" The reader immediately grasps it.

Janssens: With Nabokov you also have the delaying effect; rereading you find new things . . .

Gass: Yes indeed. But, you know, as a reader you enter into a text. For a good reader the first reading is the preparation for reading the book. People say: "yes, I have read *Moby Dick*", when they have read it the first time. Well, they haven't read *Moby Dick:* They are getting ready to read *Moby Dick.* An ideal reader has, I think, a grasp of that very fact about the depth and the complexity. You don't get it all at once, but you get a sense of what is going on. If you are reading the opening pages of, say, *Malte Laurids Brigge,* which is an incredibly good book, you don't know what it is about. All the symbols have to be worked out, but you know that the power of the page is already there implicitly. It is like meeting somebody whom you know almost at once would be an inexhaustible person. When I was in high school I started on Joyce's *Ulysses.* I ploughed my way through that book, but I knew I was in the presence of a great work. And I think that that hits you especially in poetry. You can read a poem for the first time, and it is too complex. I remember reading "Sunday Morning," Wallace Stevens' poem, for the first time, and I knew: a great poem, but could I have said what it was about? I hadn't the slightest idea. But of course you have to be a trained reader to recognize that. Something has to hit.

Janssens: Would you say something about your "work in progress"? What is in the making and what are your plans for the future?

Gass: I have a very clear program, so to speak. I have a small book which I am trying to finish that is a parallel, a companion to *On Being Blue,* called *The Soul Inside the Sentence.* It is on the nature of creativity and the nature of sentences themselves. It is a kind of pseudo-critical work on what gives sentences their character and their power, and what constitutes a sentence that is artistically powerful.

Janssens: Is it an extension of your work on Gertrude Stein?

Gass: Yes. I want to develop first of all a theory about the motivation for writing such sentences. Of course, your natural examples then come not from fiction but from essayists and writers like Sir Thomas Browne, because this language is not telling a story; nobody believes any of the facts. Similarly, with, say, *The Anatomy of Melancholy,* there is no intrusion of: is this true?—there is no intrusion of: where is the story? And Donne's Sermons (o.k. Donne meant what he was saying, he was talking about God and all the rest, but we don't have to worry about that). It is in fact the watching of the development, poetically, of ideas. Well, anyway, that book I hope to finish this summer. I am well under way. It involves also the new conceptions of aesthetic form in a sentence, how it differs from syntactical and grammatical forms, logical forms, from indeed a number of other kinds of forms which might and have been attributed to sentences by linguists. So it will involve a certain amount of technical stuff. Then I want to finish the novel; that's next on the list.

Janssens: You once said that your natural scope in whatever genre, fiction or essay, was about 40 pages.

Gass: Yes. It has in fact turned out that the sections of the novel will run forty to fifty pages. You may recall in a story I wrote, "In the Heart of the Heart of the Country," there were these sections. In the novel the sections are all about the same length: forty-page sections, and they have little titles which both refer to the old-fashioned way of putting little titles to chapters—you know: "Jack discovers his money is gone," or something—but also then orchestrate the whole text in these sections in a way somewhat like in "In the Heart of the Heart of the Country."

Janssens: Will it be the sort of novel, as you sometimes put it, you read in rather than read through?

Gass: Yes, but it is also of course meant to be read through. I really want to orchestrate it, so that there is a build-up, a tension; so going through will be important to the experience of the book, if you are going to get the thing as I am hoping to do it. On the other hand, because of the complexity of it, it is going to be for the reader, as it is designed in the structure of the work, like digging a tunnel. There will be lots of times when the reader says: "to hell with it" and stops digging. There are going to be cave-ins, you know; and points at which the tunnel, which the narrator wants to keep hidden, is discovered and you have to start somewhere else. In other words, the tunnel is also the metaphor for the book.

Janssens: You are very, interested in architecture. For sometime now you have been working in close association with the New York architect Peter Eisenman. First, do you see any relation between your interest in architecture and in literature?

Gass: A close one, I think. What one does often when one is constructing a story is to have a kind of metaphorical model for the story which may have a great deal to do with the structure of it. For instance, a story that I have gone over very carefully recently, Katherine Anne Porter's "The Grave," is a story that has a clear metaphorical model. The story is also a grave. The title of the story is a headstone. The grave in the story is discovered by two children who enter it and discover objects in it and so on. It stands for the unconscious memory suddenly coming back, and there is an epiphany at the end. It is clear, then, that the story has a model which is governing the story itself, a metaphor outside itself in a way, and, as I said before; my novel, *The Tunnel* is a tunnel in a certain metaphorical sense. But then there is a whole notion of the metaphor for a book that is not just some particular story but the idea of all books, or all kinds of texts, and for me that is very much architectural. James made the same kind of discrimination, for his metaphors were often painting metaphors—so you painted a scene and you rendered a character in a sense of portraits—but when he went to talk about the overall structure, it was always architecture; it shifted the image. Now, the idea of a book as fundamentally or conceptually a structure in which you are being taken on a tour by the author—I think a lot of modern works are constructed this way. Joyce, for instance, makes *Ulysses* in such a way that it is not possible for you to conceive the book and hold it in your head at the same time; you have to go back and forth in it. He takes you through the first time; you may jump around in it later as you wish—and *Finnegans Wake* is certainly constructed that way. For me a book tends to exist in a metaphorical relationship to a building. For me architecture represents best the basic metaphorical image of the way a text exists, say, metaphysically or philosophically. I have to read a house the way I read a book, because I cannot get it all at once. It is linear, because this house exists all at once, but cannot be perceived by me or experienced by me all at once.

Janssens: Do you use the word linear here in the same sense as you used it earlier?

Gass: I experience it linearly in the sense that I can only experience one thing after the other; I experience it serially, linear fashion. Then I hold things in my mind; I remember what is alike when I am in one part of the building, but there are other parts, just as I remember a part of *Tom Jones* in a later part of *Tom Jones*. The difference, of course, in a book is that presumably I am driven in one direction only made by the text going along. But you can also construct a work on the idea that although you can go through it, in a certain fashion you can look back and go back and forth and have a spatial relationship to it, although you experience it in a linear fashion. So what I like about that aspect is that it encompasses some of the levels of existence of a literary work—one of which is the temporal, serial order of experiencing it—but then there is the whole notion of the remembering of the work, going back, rereading and establishing different kinds of relationships of that sort, and ultimately the notion, of course, that the whole book exists all at once. It is not like a piece of music in one sense; that is, if I am listening to a piece of music I cannot just jump ahead and catch the end—of course a tape recorder is something else—but I can with a book; I can just flip ahead, I can go back.

Janssens: Yes, certain books make you do this, but *Tom Jones,* for instance, is constructed differently. At the end Fielding gives you blank chapter
headings because he wants to keep all the clues to himself and wants all the
fun and excitement to be in the telling.

Gass: That's true. All texts exist in this way for Fielding, or for Richardson, and you are not even expected to have a complete and total memory.
They don't expect you to remember at page 500 everything that happened on
page 1, whereas Joyce does; that is, Joyce demands a total recall, an ideal
total recall, so there is a conceptual notion of the way the text exists in Joyce
that is fundamentally different from Fielding, although for both physical
print, or what I like to call the inscriptional order, has to be the same. But in
reading I don't go continuously, I break off, I take up the book a week later,
I go back and forth. I am like I would be when I went through a building: I
am putting the pieces together to compose the building which exists ontologi-
cally all at the same time, and which I can only know experientially one at
the time, and therefore I can only conceive or conceptualize the way it actually exists; I can have an idea of how this house exists. Now in Peter Eisenman's work, what he wants to do often is to make one experientially aware
of other parts of the house at the same time. So in one of his houses, called
House Six, there is, for instance, in the second-floor bedroom a strip of glass
that goes across the floor, from which you can perceive the living-room
below, and vice versa. Similarly, there are holes in various parts, openings
which allow you—the way in which I can look, say, through a house through
a stairwell—to took through the house. So I am always aware in that house
of other parts. Well now, in "The Menelaiad," when Barth opens up cuts in
the story through the fact that something is said, let us say, in one of the
many layers of the story, suddenly there'll be an opening; something is said
in one story which is also said in all the others, and it's just as if you were
seeing right through all of the floors, the stories; and it is, of course, constructed this way. So Eisenman realizes that although the ontological way in
which a building exists is simultaneous, the experiential character of a building is always temporal. Furthermore, he gets interested in a play between the
way the building came into being as a building in the development of its
logic, and the way in which the experiencer of the building comes to grasp
it. So for me the architectural analogy—it is only an analogy—is a very very
strong one.

Janssens: Would you say, something about your joint ventures with Peter
Eisenman. The first, I gather, is now at the printer's?

Gass: Yes, that's done. Peter is now in the process of designing the book, and Godine has already accepted it. The text is done and it'll be a Godine spring book. And it is going to be the most outrageous book ever put together: Peter will make sure of that. And it'll be wonderful. He does crazy things in one sense, but he is really a serious artist, first rank, I think. He is not just doing things to shock people, or surprise them or be different. And then this latest thing that we are considering. He came to me and said: you know, after this present thing is done, I'd like to design a house for you, and of course, it would be an imaginary house in the sense that it would not be built, but it would be a house. So I said: it might be interesting, instead of designing a house for me, as it is going to be an imaginary house in a way, why not design the house for a character in a story? I'll write the story and you design the house for the character. I think my story will be more directive, because in a sense it is the program, and then his house is designed to the program. But there will be an interchange; just as if I take my ideas to an architect and he starts making plans, I'm going to start changing my ideas. I think it is an interesting notion even if nothing comes of it. I am all set to write this thing.

Janssens: Have you always been so conscious of the execution of your design in your stories and essays, or has the writing been more of a process where you have felt your way . . .

Gass: I know that dimly I want to get something of a certain sort, but I don't know what the hell it is. I mean, it takes me a long time to find out, and that is the critical thing. Once you get that sense of the kind of thing that you are making, it really becomes a making. I think the Greek derivation for poetry is just right: it is a making, really constructing something. One of the critical problems, I think, for writers is the abstractness of the medium, just as for an architect it is the opposite, except in Eisenman's sort of work which is almost purely conceptual. For him the material is almost irrelevant; all it needs to do is to express the architectural ideas, so that is why I call it cardboard architecture, like these cardboard things you make a house out of; it is the model. When I started to think seriously about architecture in the last couple of years, I came to realize that an enormous amount of architecture is done at a conceptual, graphic level, and not at the building level at all. There are enormously influential designs which have never been put up, never will be put up, and indeed a great deal of architecture consists of that. I just had not been conscious of this sufficiently. And this of course then means that architecture is almost immediately an art of inscription, of signs—a score.

Now in Eisenman's case, who is going to put up his buildings? But even with Wright. Some of Wright's most astounding designs were never built. The mile-high skyscraper, for example: he designed a mile-high skyscraper for Chicago built like a tree with roots going very deep down, and it is a mile in the air; and this was designed, what, two decades ago, something like that, an enormously influential work. Or the glass skyscraper that Mies suggested in his youth that never got built, an enormous influence on his later work and on that of all kind of other people.

Janssens: How do you visualize *The Tunnel*?

Gass: It is going to be really difficult to set. One of the problems in that book is the problem of new inscriptional devices. That is one of the things that gets neglected, I think. In the book I am doing on the structure of the sentence a great problem is finding a way to symbolize the structures. That will almost be the same as discovery: giving the right symbolization, the right notation. Well, one gets a new musical notation and that revolutionizes music; they get an accurate dance notation and that will do the same for dance, and so forth. There are revolutions in architecture because of xeroxing processes that allow you new ways of symbolizing your architectural conceptions. Now for *The Tunnel* I want a very complex physical structure, and there are all kind of things I want to have happening. I want to have one word repeating—like a drum or a beat or a ground bass or something—repeating all through a whole page. You can of course say to the reader: that's what I want, but that won't do; you have got to get something that immediately gets the reader to hear it, not just say: oh, Gass wants this to be repeated all the time. It is great problem. Suppose what you want to do is to get the reader to pause. Instead the reader replaces conceptual notions of the pause, he does not perform the rest, goes full tilt. You got to have them perform it; that means the notation must do more than convey the idea.

Janssens: Could you give an example of what would be successful inscriptional devices or graphic arrangements?

Gass: Well, you take an ordinary passage which you write, a nice little sweet thing, and then you throw it into German print, you know that old Gothic. It changes the tone of the passage. In *Willie Masters' Lonesome Wife* most of that stuff did not work very well, but I thought that one of the things that worked best was where I put a piece of dialogue, which I took from a Walter Scott novel, in a balloon, like a cartoon, and it just fits so perfectly that it becomes a critical commentary on Scott's dialogue. It is just fit for the comic strip—well, at least that bit was. I've got a whole series of limericks in *The Tunnel,* fifty limericks of nuns, all beginning with the first line: "I once went to bed with a nun." One of these limericks shows all the positions that you went through when you went to bed with a nun, and the last position means that the last line of the limerick has to be a circle. Well, you try to figure out how different things will work, and you don't want it to be a gimmick.

Janssens: When do you think you will be done with *The Tunnel*?

Gass: A couple more years. I keep saying that but I think now I have got a very clear idea of the structure of the thing, what I want to do with it: the conception that just as the character is digging the tunnel and faces the problem of disposing of the dirt, so on the metaphorical level the reader collects material, dirt—and I like saying it is dirt—that is taken out of the language when he tunnels through the book.

Janssens: Is there a question you would have liked me to have asked?

Gass: I don't really think so. It is strange I guess. People get confused about this. I have nothing I want to tell anybody. But one is teaching or lecturing—or opposing views—the arguments with somebody like John Gardner—and the impression you are distinctly getting is that I want to persuade people of something, that I have some message. But the views that I have and formulate are mainly called for. I am constantly amazed by certain authors who feel that they must tell the world something, when what they have to tell the world is, you know, as old-fashioned and confused as: "the sky is falling down", or: "gee, life is hard . . ." I have really no interest in persuading anybody. I have no sense of having something to tell somebody, and I suppose that is what I want to tell people.

An Interview with William Gass

Jan Garden Castro / 1981

From the *ADE Bulletin,* No. 70, 1981, 30–34. Reprinted by permission of the Modern Language Association of America.

Jan Castro: Professor Gass, what is the relation between teaching and writing in your life?

William Gass: For me I think there's a very close relation. One of the things teaching does is relieve me of the sense of need for an audience in my writing, because I do have audiences all the time. I don't feel as some writers might, sort of shut off and completely away from everything. Both in writing fiction and in teaching, I go over a lot of the same material, although one is doing quite different things to it. And in some degree, too, teaching is theater, so you're moving from fiction to drama.

Castro: You say you have a small audience as a writer. Your works are very complex and deeply thought. Do you think that future readers will find them more accessible?

Gass: If one has future readers, that usually happens. I don't think they're inaccessible now. Readers don't want difficult works—not just mine—anybody's. The reward for the time, effort, agony of getting into some of these things is always problematic. It isn't simply that I have a small audience. Most of the writers I admire don't really have much of an audience.

Castro: It seems to me that you're one of the most humane and gracious teachers I've ever met, and I'm just curious about why I don't see those traits in your characters.

Gass: Well, teaching is a different enterprise. I don't believe in the novel that teaches. When you're teaching, you're engaged with something other than yourself. When you're writing novels, you're bringing things mainly out of yourself. You may be trying to make something that's not autobiographical or self-reflective, but it's made out of your character like a cake from flour. The consciousness it constructs may not be your everyday consciousness; nevertheless, it comes from your depths and not someone else's. Whereas when you're teaching you're engaged with texts; it's a different kind of thing, and your attitude as an individual toward the material that you're dealing

71

with has to be deep and warm. You're the teacher; you've got to be in love with the stuff on your syllabus.

Castro: You said in your Philosophy and Literature class that you are interested in the art of sermons and the art of preaching. Is there any relation between sermons and your own teaching style?

Gass: I think there is in the sense that preaching takes place on a public platform and involves projection, and it involves, I think, ordinary lecturing, too. The main thing you can project to students, aside from the obvious things concerning clarity and explication, is the relation that the person who's lecturing has to the material. What you do is establish—and this is similar to the sermon—a model for your involvement. That involvement can be, as it is in my case mostly, detached. I'm not a partisan. But you try to convey the importance of your closeness to your subject. I think that that isn't exactly taught to the student; it is exemplified. You can have a chance, of course, to introduce people to wonderful things, but then you have to treat those wonderful things in such a way that they stay wonderful. You can't kill them.

Castro: Exactly. Another professor was saying to me that it's anathema to be condescending about drawing conclusions for the student.
Gass: Yes, indeed.

Castro: When you studied with Wittgenstein at Cornell, how did he influence you?
Gass: What Wittgenstein taught me in that short period was not so much any of his conclusions or ideas, which I was thoroughly familiar with before I ever saw him; it was his involvement, his commitment to his meaning. The intellectual integrity he displayed was awesome, absolutely. I was watching not just a really great mind in operation but also an absolutely honest and pure intellect. I don't think he was an honest and pure person, but he had that intellect, and you saw it. It was like seeing a great artist in operation— absolute scruple. No second rate stuff would be permitted. That was really impressive. Again, it was an exemplification. Socrates embodies that way; I'm sure Spinoza must have. And Wittgenstein was the complete embodiment of that quest in himself.

Castro: Could you explain a statement you made in a *Colorado State Review* interview: "I'm a Platonist in my aesthetic; that is, I want to treat language as a Platonist would treat forms, but I'm not a Platonist outside, philosophically."

Gass: What I mean by that is that a great many philosophical theories about the world seem to me false, but if you take them and apply them to the made-up worlds of fiction, they're often true. They describe what the world ought to be like in a perfect novel. And Plato's attitude toward language is ideal for the creation of fictional things, but I don't think Plato's view of the real world is correct. It's odd, but by and large the rationalist philosophers tend to be quite accurate in setting standards for an aesthetic appreciation of a world that is made-up. But I think the empiricists are right in the way they describe what is actually the case. I enjoy reading the rationalists far more than the empiricists, because the rationalists are concerned with their system holding together; they are concerned with the almost independent development of concepts, which is what one does when one writes. They tend to be nonrepresentational, which is what I like in art. I'm not interested in representing the world. If I wanted to do that, I'd be in sociology or science or something.

Castro: In your art, what are you interested in?

Gass: I'm interested in making a self-contained system of concepts, ideas that will then define a kind of consciousness. It's a way of inventing a consciousness by supplying someone with the structure and content of an experience. So I make that up and create that consciousness. It's not a consciousness *of* the world; it's a consciousness *of* the work.

Castro: You were talking in class today about the author's mind and the author's persona's mind, and the persona sometimes taking over in the creation of the work. So whose consciousness is in the creation of the work?

Gass: What you've got to do is make a work that contains its own rules and structures. Certainly your own consciousness is going to be reflected, but you're going to make a consciousness that you may not have as a part of your ordinary lift. You don't necessarily apprehend the world in the way you're asking that things be apprehended in your book. For instance, I regard the world as largely a matter of chance and, fundamentally, of deep confusion. In my work, although I might want to give that appearance at times, everything has to be ordered and arranged and have reasons and so forth. In life, I don't think there are reasons for much. But in the work you can explain everything. The fiction and art I enjoy does not seem generally accurate about life. What it of course does do is reflect what many philosophers wish for the world.

Castro: In English and philosophy departments, this an increasing amount of jargon and of technical research, and so one criticism of these departments is that their work is increasingly esoteric and irrelevant.

Gass: That's really true of all subjects. Consider the difficulty. I don't have any desire to support or defend unimportant exercises. The problem is, when you're trying to teach people a subject and to make a deep investigation of something, it is often necessary to invent new terminology and to penetrate matters in a way that looks minute and trivial at first. Now, when those exercises fail, you've got just this great rubbish heap. And one is inclined to say, "We shouldn't be doing this." But it's not that. It's that we should be doing it well. And the only way to teach anybody eventually how to write is to do a lot of analysis and probing, and most of it's going to be bad. It depends on how it's done. Specialization is dangerous only when we fail to understand what real specialization is. For instance, if I'm a specialist in Chaucer, then that means I'm going to enter the language so completely that the deeper I get into Chaucer, the more I'm going to realize I have to understand about everything else in order to understand Chaucer. The same thing happens in philosophy. The more you take some issue-let's suppose it's a technical issue in logic-and start pushing it, the more you see that you can't understand that issue unless you understand the whole of logic and then pretty soon all of philosophy, and it goes on and on.

The same is true through the other side of it. In most academic fields we have two kinds of courses, so to speak: the heavily specialized and the genial general survey. They are often at odds. Then again, the survey course is useless unless the people involved in putting it together know what happens when you look at things from a plane. Every generalist has to be a specialist about something. I think you realize that to be a good specialist you have to be a generalist. In the long run they cover the same ground; they just go at it differently.

Castro: How does time affect language?

Gass: An enormous sort of a cruel silting up takes place. It's wonderful to get students excited about the history of words so that they have a sense for the depth in them, the changes that occur, and the meanings that accrue. You are dealing, in language, with geological objects. They really do have strata, they have histories, and you can bring those to the surface and work with them, sometimes change them. To the degree that you happen to be rather mystical about it, you can regard your language as working fundamentally at the depths of a past that even you aren't quite aware of consciously. Words' histories are solidifications of everything people have thought about certain things, yet we're used to using them to order breakfast. When writing, however, one is often working at a depth that one is not able to touch consciously. Every word is a relic. The fact that words have dates and ages is marvelous because you can juxtapose new words with old, conscious that a sentence is a collection of these creatures. Some are at different distances like the stars, some are snobs and have a high social status, and others are just bits of junk, weightless as Saran Wrap. But to put them together in one sentence is wonderful.

Castro: You said in the *New Fiction* interview that painting has influenced your theory of art and music has influenced your practice of it.

Gass: I tend to treat literature spatially more than temporally. My image of a book is something created as a whole, as a complete thing, but one that can be apprehended a bit at a time. I suppose the closest thing to it would be a large tapestry or a Chinese scroll you unwind; so it's a painting that you can't see all at once. The tapestry is, in fact, the model for Rilke's great novel *The Notebooks of Malte Laurids Brigge,* but it's so big you can't see it all at once. Nonetheless, it's *there* all at once, and the effect of it is like the blow of a rock. I think a great novel—or any great work—affects one as a whole. That's true of music too. That is, you see a piece of music not as a series of fragments marching on but as squads and companies and battalions of an army. So our image of a work in literature is of the completed book. It exists very much like a piece of architecture. Now, this building we're in exists in its entirety, but I can never experience all of it at once; I have to travel through it. Similarly with a book. I have to travel through the book, but the text is there as a whole.

Castro: And your technique, you have said, is to build it bit by bit.

Gass: When I'm practicing writing, I'm not visually oriented but auditory, so the writing of it—word by word, line by line—is done by ear, and in that sense music is the dominant art. You actually have both elements: the linear, serial problem—literature does unfold one word at a time—but the completed object has to be conceived as a whole. Those two aspects are interacting, and there's really a tension between them that can be used.

Castro: I'm "hearing" both the sounds of words and musical modes. Have you used any musical modes? Some writers have said they use a fugal structure.

Gass: I've used a fugue, literally, in a story called "The Pedersen Kid," and it is, of course, a question of constructing a round. More often I think in terms of recursiveness, of repetitive patterns, of sonata forms—those in which you start out, return, start out come back again.

Castro: The timing, the measure.

Gass: Including scansion, all things that have to do with prosody. A lot of rhetorical structures are musical, with their parallelisms and so on. There is also the possibility of carrying on many voices-of polyphony. Most of my own images come, I think, from opera. I have a fondness for the catalogue aria. Often too, I find myself talking about things in poetic forms. This stanza, I'll say to myself, is giving me trouble, instead of this paragraph. I think: this aria, this duet.

Castro: In the *Colorado State Review* interview, you said: "Most novelists are still concerned with content, with truth. I'm only concerned with beauty." What is beauty for you when you start to write? In a letter to your publisher, you once said that the middle of *Omensetter* is gross and that you considered Reverend Jethro Furber's twisted Biblical sermons the best writing you had done up to that point. So what is beauty?

Gass: There is a view that some ideas are so obnoxious that they can't be put into a form that would be rather beautiful. Some believe there is a conflict between, for example, moral value and aesthetic value, such that viciousness can't be beautiful. I claim it can. One way of doing that is to demonstrate it. It is perfectly possible, it seems to me, for there to be a beautiful anti-Semitic speech. My present work requires me to do just that. So some of it is the challenge of creating something out of garbage, and there's a philosophical point there if you can make it. But also, the words are nothing by themselves until they're placed in relationships. For me, there are no bad words; there are just ill-written things. So the idea is to find contexts so integrated and interconnected that they have the beauty some mathematicians speak of. Everything fits. Everything's functioning fully. You have a complete system. It's sometimes a challenge to make that system out of things people find rather awful or objectionable. It's careless to associate what the characters say with what the author thinks. I frequently don't agree with what mine say. The challenge is, to me, to be able to say it as well as I can and represent and fit it into the larger scheme. It doesn't matter whether what I'm saying is nice or true.

Castro: This is a very important issue because there are many levels of interpretation. There is what the writer thinks he or she is saying, what the persona is saying, what the reader *thinks is* happening, and so forth. I have a question in this regard about Omensetter in *Omensetter's Luck.* You said in the *New Fiction* interview that the point is that the novel isn't really set in Ohio and that characters such as Omensetter who live lucky, natural lives don't exist; you conclude: "Beliefs lost are minds cleaned. I applaud the development." I *read* something else: it is significant that in the novel other people's views of Omensetter often become more tangible than the character. My question is two-fold: one, are you knocking down a straw horse, a figure that never existed? two, Omensetter leaves town in good health, scot-free, after much trumped-up trouble from the rabid Reverend, so what is there to cause the reader to lose any belief in, or liking for, Omensetter?

Gass: Omensetter is simply a polarization of dreams or myths. The natural man is a common myth in American literature. People just used Omensetter as a screen on which to project their own desires. You're quite right; Omensetter is not really tangible, because he rarely appears as himself. He has no self, only what others give him. It isn't, then, that people have a clear view of Omensetter; he's just somebody who apparently arouses those projections in people, for better or worse. He's not seen for himself at all. Who knows who he is? The idea that he is a happy person is something that is projected too. On the other hand, I am not using the book to argue against any of these views. That's just something that happens in the book. The fact that I happen to believe that there aren't any naturally happy people in that sense, that it's a myth, doesn't matter.

Castro: You have published portions of *The Tunnel,* a novel you said you have been writing since 1965. The book has a narrator you've described as extremely bitter. Is he to be trusted? Does he exist in the American landscape as the Socratic accuser who speaks the truth or as a liar who slanders and debunks?

Gass: He's both. He is a liar, and he does slander and debunk, but he represents a basic type. I want him to be a combination of things, not just a liar. He's a truth teller too. He's a puritan and a sensualist, stupid and bright; he's everyman in a way. But I don't think every man would like him as a picture of everyman. He's a monster. I don't think, as a monster, he's any different from anybody else. Often what other people take for madness, I take for the normal.

Castro: What would the purpose of such a character be?

Gass: I'm not trying to preach what is true about people; I just happen to think that people will be, in fact, more like this character than they're prepared to admit. I don't care. I'm just inventing the character. I am afraid that I will be identified with him and I'm taking some risks there. But this character does represent, I think, what becomes of people who are fundamentally disillusioned and disappointed, who have promise and have reason for promise and are deeply disappointed. I'm conducting a fictional, not an actual, investigation into fascist crime.

Castro: Why create a fascist? Why not a Socratic person?

Gass: Because I want to contaminate. I want to show what happens when virtue is in a mind of a certain sort. Some things you can put in a sinkhole and they're destroyed—but if I drop a silver dollar in the garbage, I can just pick it out. What I want to create is an environment where you can test those very things.

Castro: In *Willie Masters' Lonesome Wife,* the lady is not any one person; she is representing what has happened to language as it is used.

Gass: She is language in a way. She speaks for it and embodies it. And that's how she grows and gets her character. In other words, she comes out of a metaphor. If language is the medium, then I can set up the standard relation of the author to the medium as to a lover or a prostitute or whatever. And you really have to make her a kind of prostitute because language is available to anybody. She is a character who emerges only to express an abstraction. There is no person.

Castro: You have said that metaphor is central to our understanding and use of language, that language is metaphor. Could you explain the ways it is metaphorical?

Gass: If there is anything in writing that comes easy for me it's making up metaphors. They just appear. I can't move two lines without all kinds of images. Then the problem is how to make the best of them. In its geological character, language is almost invariably metaphorical. That's how meanings tend to change. Words become metaphors for other things, then slowly disappear into the new image. I have a hunch, too, that the core of creativity is located in metaphor, in model making, really. A novel is a large metaphor for the world. I'm working on an essay right now involving this question of what the relation of a work of fiction to the world of nonfiction is. Novels obviously are about the world in some way. What I'm suggesting in this piece is that novels are about the world metaphorically and that they stand to their world of rhetoric the way a scientific model stands to its world of mathematics. Fictional and scientific systems have different uses, but I think they're made in certain similar ways. I'm trying to argue that.

Castro: There are many reports coming out now, including the Rockefeller Report, *The Humanities of American Life,* on the future of the humanities and literary study. What is the future of literature and philosophy, in your opinion?

Gass: It's hard to say, depending on whether you mean the remote future or the immediate future. The immediate future is grim on all counts because of the loss of job opportunities and funding, the decline of interest in the humanities. One could go on. Also, there is the legacy of overspecialization, of overexpanded departments, of professors who think it's natural for an academic to go to Europe every couple of years. Alas. Nothing natural there. We had a decade of Great Times. Faculty members in universities—in the past—were paid well; they've got to get used to going back to being honest, poor people again. There's going to be a period of disillusionment and grim decisions. Simply—salaries are going to shrink. We're going to have a hold-over of spoiled, knuckleheaded, narrow-minded scholars teaching increasingly timorous and inadequate students who worry mostly about their next buck and not about Truth or Beauty. Well, all of that, I think, seems reasonable in the immediate future. But at the same time, even if that happens, it's in a way a good thing, because our graduate programs are too large. Philosophy should always be small. There shouldn't be a lot of people wanting to be philosophers; it makes no sense. Furthermore, this kind of procedure will eliminate all the good-time Charlies and we'll have only dedicated people. The shrinkage process has its advantages.

The other, larger problem, of course, is what the impact of, the humanities on life is going to be. I think we are going to feel their presence less and less. And of course that's unfortunate, but I am not, like some of my colleagues on the commission, surprised by this. The humanities have rarely been important in the United States and will never become important. I think they should be important, but they're not going to be. Writing is not important either.

Castro: What is the relation of the humanities to society?

Gass: We must try to get people to think further than their guts and genitals—to appreciate values—but this can be done best only in the primary and secondary schools. By the time you get to the university, it's almost too late. By and large, you can't do anything to change society in a college classroom. I think universities should and *can* take more leadership in trying to strengthen not just the humanities but every area of education at the primary and secondary level.

Castro: In Missouri, there are already state cutbacks on funds, the elimination of the Artist-in-Schools program, and some school closings.

Gass: The situation is very grim. In a way we know what has to be done, and we know how very unlikely getting it done is. In fact, the parents don't want their kids to have a liberal education. The kids don't want it. The politicians don't want it. Nobody wants it. They don't believe in it. They don't even understand it. Partly that's the humanists' fault, no question about it. But I don't think the humanists simply by themselves are going to be able to change much. You do what you can.

An Interview with William Gass

Arthur M. Saltzman / 1984

From *Contemporary Literature*, 25.2, 121–35. © 1984. Reprinted by permission of the University of Wisconsin Press.

William Gass's upstairs study struck me as an extratextual equivalent for the self-contained world of words that is so prominent a theme in his writing: books covered three walls and stood in waist-high stacks on the floor, prompting Gass, who was dressed to accommodate a typically stifling summer day in St. Louis, to apologize for his peculiar manner of "insulating" his home. As Gass spoke about his fiction, his speculative essays, and his thoughts regarding their interrelationship, he seemed to be tapping into an ongoing process of self-scrutiny. The author is clearly his own most diligent critic. As he does in his writing, Gass shaped his answers with precision and care, befitting his belief that the word is a formidable event in its own right, and that "language is the vehicle of the upper self."

Both as an essayist and as a writer of fiction, William Gass has earned the reputation of being one of the most accomplished stylists of his generation. He is a principal advocate of the central importance in literature of the physical, even erotic, qualities of language—"the soul inside the sentence"—and of the self-referential integrity of the literary text. A professor of philosophy at Washington University, Gass has consistently argued that language undergoes an ontological change when it is incorporated into literature, while the notion of a realistic imagination is an oxymoron that prevents us from appreciating the literary achievement for what it is: the creation of a verbal object that is not a description of reality but an addition to it. Gass has also won notoriety as a practitioner of and a spokesman for technical experimentation in recent American fiction, staunchly defending the aesthetic and moral value of innovative form.

Gass's criticism is represented by two influential collections, *Fiction and the Figures of Life* (1970) and *The World within the Word* (1978), and by the extended philosophical inquiry, *On Being Blue* (1976), a highly poetic rumination on the nature of color, sexuality, and the reading process. His fiction includes a novel, *Omensetter's Luck* (1966), which may be read as an intricately textured reassessment of many of the fundamental themes of American literature; a pioneering collection of stories, *In the Heart of the Heart of the Country* (1968); the relentlessly metafictional *Willie Masters' Lonesome Wife* (1971), a multi-generic, typographically playful investigation of literary language itself; and several sections of a mammoth work-in progress, *The Tunnel,* which have appeared in a variety of periodicals over the past fifteen years.

Q.: In 1981 you did an interview with Jan Garden Castro in which you said that beauty and morality are aspects of form rather than of belief, and what matters is that what you say is well said, not whether it is attractive or true. I am wondering where a writer's beliefs do belong in his art. Is having a point to make about the world a valid reason for writing fiction? Certainly there are many novelists who hope to teach us something about the world. Is that desire applicable to the way literature affects us?

A.: Certainly that's a motive for writing, but I don't think it's enough to justify it. There are lots of personal reasons why one writes, and they may include a message or attitude or self-expression—there are millions of possibilities, but these exist for people who are not writing, too. Now the question is whether or not you can succeed in forming your opinions or attitudes in such a way that they are artistically interesting. When that's done, they become artistically viable even if people don't share them and are not persuaded. In fact, the more you tend to make your opinions artistically interesting, the less rhetorical effectiveness they tend to have. They tend to get distanced and to become objects of contemplation, not belief.

Q.: One of the problems I have in coming to terms with the primacy of the word over the conviction is knowing what to do with artists who are generally accepted as important, even great, but who perhaps are not so stylistically elegant. Dreiser, for example.

A.: I don't think Dreiser is worth bothering with, except as a social phenomenon. He's certainly historically important, and expressive of ideas and attitudes and interests, but he can't write. Again, there are two elements here. There is the notion of a construction that you might talk about somewhat independently of the particular words used to form a story like *An American Tragedy.* But for my money, work like that, as opposed, say, to Trollope or someone else whose writing, while it may not be line-by-line distinguished, is nuanced and careful and has constructions of interest . . . I don't find much of that in someone like Dreiser.

Q.: I'm going to paraphrase you now. An author's responsibility is to the coherence of his system. As this theory applies to *Omensetter's Luck,* what is it that leads to Furber's breakdown in that novel? Is it that his system is somehow fractured by contact with Omensetter, or are there imperfections inherent in the system that confrontation with Omensetter merely emphasizes or brings to light?

A.: Oh, yes, the latter, certainly. And of course, Furber is confronted by the fact that his own system of ideas might really be true. I mean, it was okay to believe it as long as it really *wasn't so.* That's true for a lot of people. Beliefs are held in a very strange way. We notice the contradictions in people's behaviors—they believe this and they do that, so that you can measure differences. For instance, I believe that fire burns, and so I don't put my hand in it. I believe that there is a God, but then I do all kinds of things which suggest that my belief, even though it's deeply held, is a different kind of thing. I think that if something happened to make people believe that there was a God, *really,* then the confrontation with the consequences of that would be terrifying. I mean, if there really were a Being controlling the world, look what this Being is doing! What happens to Furber is that his rhetoric is brought home. It was tolerable as long as it was held in rhetorical abeyance, but as soon as it becomes more than that, it becomes intolerable.

Q.: What happens when you have a character who has the capacity for imposing his rhetorical constructions on the world?

A.: That is, of course, what everybody does, it seems to me. Furber is just very good at it. He's aware of it, and he tries to slip by problems by creating more rhetoric. And there's a point at which he's unable to do that . . . because he's confronted by somebody who apparently has no rhetoric at all.

Q.: You've mentioned elsewhere that Furber was your hero, or at least your main character, because he's the one with the language. The hero is the one with the good lines. Is that the case with all literature?

A.: Yes. In this inverted way, Furber is the hero, though not in any ordinary sense. He is certainly the central, pivotal character because he has the best lines, and people have been puzzled about that because it moves him toward a heroic status. I was just reading a book on the origins of eloquence—it was talking about the Elizabethan period—and the point being made in that book is that a great many of the dramatic moments in Shakespeare, for example, succeed mainly because the rhetoric succeeds. Psychological shifts, changes of heart, all sorts of things happen which are inexplicable, except that if the speech is good enough, it works. The same thing is true in the way I go at things.

Q.: What is it that finally separates Gass the artist from Furber the artist, or from the other obsessive, rhetorically, minded characters in your work?

A.: The differentiation has to do with whether or not an author can take characters with varying points of view and lend them appropriate language. If he couldn't, then one would have to ask if this is a character or if this is the author, because the author hasn't given a language to a character, but just tacked a character's name on his own language. That's a problem I have in the novel I'm working on presently. There's only one character. All the language belongs to that character. And yet, certain characters have to emerge, with language intact, within that system. That's simply an explicit statement of what's a hidden problem when the author is not present but is creating characters. Here the narrator is present and is creating characters.

Q.: Even though they are attractive by virtue of their language, many of your most effective characters are not attractive personally.

A.: No, the narrator of the new novel is not.

Q.: You've spoken of Satan before, and of Iago, and of the fascination of evil. You are drawn to it in your own writing as well. Does that suggest a pessimistic view of the world, or is it rather that Nazism in *The Tunnel* is interesting as a formal challenge, as an organizational structure.

A.: Both of those things are the case. I actually was working this morning on just that idea. The superior importance of evil, in the sense that that's what we really believe in. The rhetorical stance I was taking, or giving to the character, was that there are no heroes we can really believe in anymore, but we do believe in our villains.

Q.: They are more substantial, somehow.

A.: Yes, and more knowledge will not take our dislike of Attila the Hun or Hitler away. In fact, what is going to be bad about my narrator's problem is that I have probably written a book in which he sees some good in Hitler, which is inexcusable. To see some bad in Albert Schweitzer is usual. What I have the narrator start talking about is evil's greater stature in our reality. As a writer, I've overextended the case. I'm giving it to Kohler—he is thinking this, uttering the cynicism of an extreme character—but I hope I know what the weaknesses of those arguments are, and can back off and undercut them if I need to. But I've got to make that seem convincing for the reader at the time. Otherwise, the character doesn't seem to be feeling these things.

Q.: Is *The Tunnel* near completion?

A.: It's coming along pretty well now. I know what its structure is, how long it's going to be. Most of the things are laid out. It's a matter of finally executing them, a matter of staying in the book continuously for maybe another year.

Q.: You've spoken of "character" several times, and I wonder if terms such as "character" and "plot" retain their relevance in your literary theory. What happens to them once we see a novel as a self contained referential system? Do such traditional means of evaluating fiction still hold up?

A.: They get redefined. I don't think they drop out at all. There are levels of structure in which those things are very important. For me, a character is really a voice and a source of language. If one has really created a character, then he knows that that character is going to have its language and will be speaking in a certain way. Words are going to come out from that source either as direct speech or as a means of dictating the language you use in the third person to describe scenes or that individual from outside. It starts giving you the words, the gestures, everything. It's a source of language. Although I don't write like Stanley Elkin at all, I think that what Stanley does is something a lot of us do, and that is find a voice. But I think what Stanley does is find an occupation and then let the occupation speak. That occupation creates a voice, which then creates a character, and gives him his book.

Q.: And yet for many writers, including Elkin and yourself, all the characters seem to have this propensity for highly lyrical language. I think of Henry James's housekeepers, too. It's as if this kind of writer wants to do justice to his situation by giving every character a vocabulary. Does that compromise the effect of his novel?

A.: No, that's just antirealism. In the first story I wrote, I tried to cut the vocabulary down because I had a character of a limited vocabulary. But I still wanted poetry. Now I don't try to do that. Faulkner doesn't do that. Shakespeare doesn't do it. Dickens doesn't do it. It is perfectly legitimate to make that restriction as a formal problem. You could do it if you wanted to. But it doesn't seem in any way necessary. You can choose to release your language for all your characters, or you can decide to restrict it in certain ways. Both are perfectly reasonable decisions of a thoroughly technical sort.

To say a plumber must speak in a certain way is part of a tradition that you can accept. But it's only a convention.

Q.: In a recent essay of yours, "Representation and the War for Reality," you argue in part that human consciousness cannot apprehend reality without the interference of language. All mental acts are dependent upon being constructed in words before we are able to make use of them. Depending on one's point of view, language is either a barrier or a shield. It's a matter of attitude how we deal with this inevitability. I am curious to know if the beauty of the verbal world is your adequate compensation for not being able to get at the physical world more directly.

A.: No, I think it's not adequate. Art is not the solution to everything. In fact, it solves hardly anything. It may make life bearable. One of the things that's involved in the idea of *The Tunnel* is the attempt to get outside language. The fact is that language creates a world that protects us and that we can live in, but it also bamboozles us. This is also true of emotions. Love is wonderful while you're in it, but it is also illusory, and the same thing happens with language. It is certainly not adequate. I would not want to suggest that because there are beautiful things all the moral problems go away. They don't at all.

Q.: You've called literary realism a contradiction in terms. Solidity of specification, the appearance of factual reality in works of literature—are these results of mistaken impressions about what art truly is?

A.: The only real difference between literary realism, which is a perfectly legitimate mode, and formal alternatives which reject it, is that literary realists make the mistake of thinking that the world is like that, and that this justifies the constructions they make. That is a mistake. Now the real artists among the great realists didn't allow that to happen. Even now you have people like Robbe-Grillet, who is a realist—he just has a different conception of reality. He creates a world that is nothing like Dickens's, but both might think, "Ah, but this is the way it really is." Yet we will read either if they are good enough writers, not because they may happen to create a world which moves us to say it's "the real thing."

Q.: Ronald Sukenick said something to the effect that every generation's best writers see themselves as moving closer to their conception of realism, so that realism is actually a very fluid, subjective notion, even as a convention for literature. He also talks about setting himself formal tasks. He will have a guiding rhythm or metaphor for a story—an arbitrary beginning to generate language. Do you ever begin in this fashion?

A.: If it's a single short story, that choice may dominate all the way through; if it's a novel, there will be several of those choices, right down to the shaping of paragraphs. Often it's not an arbitrary choice. You start to work with a particular passage, and it hasn't got any shape. So you foist a possibility on it, and then force it. So it's an exchange. Often the passage suggests its shape, but it's not all there—you have to push. I do that constantly—page after page almost. That's one reason I'm interested in rhetorical tropes and schemes. They're really the syntax of paragraphs and longer formulas. They are ordering processes, and I couldn't get on without those things. I have an interesting exchange at times with my wife, who's an architect. When she has a new problem, like the site plan for a school she's working on now, she tends to approach the problem with all sorts of considerations, while I would come at the problem, as do many of the architects I admire, with all kinds of geometrical potentialities sitting there quite abstractly, quite independently of the problem, and the problem then gets molded. It has to squeeze itself into the abstractions, and not the other way around.

Q.: According to the terminology of "Representation and the War for Reality," does that make a "thin" rather than a "thick"?

A.: From that direction, I would be a thin, yes.

Q.: It struck me how in that article you seemed to be claiming a very definite distinction between those who favor design and those who admit data in a comparatively unqualified way. It seems that both are natural aspects of the human mind.

A.: Oh, sure. You're moving to the center position. You've got a model, but it's a matter of which end you move from, and I tend to move from the abstract end. Mary tends to move from the other. You can always tell where one arrives from.

Q.: I'm also reminded of your essay "Carrots, Noses, Snow, Rose, Roses," which says that words undergo an ontological transformation when placed in a context like a carrot in a snowman's face. I'm inclined to say, "Look at that snowman's nose. Now there's a clever use of a carrot," which doesn't let go of either end of the carrot's reality.

A.: Again, both parts of it are natural. Both are real. It's a matter of the reader's willingness to entertain that additional real claim.

Q.: You've argued that the artist's ultimate effect on society is a revolution of consciousness. This appears to be the burden of your essay "The Artist and Society." Is this a more qualified effect than what the social realist hopes to achieve?

A.: Mine is a more radical stance. Just from the sociopolitical side of it, somebody tends to be regarded as a realist if he is working in a mode that people around him recognize as Reality. If he is trying to change things, he's changing them within that system of perceiving things. He's accepting that system, buying it. He has the possibility of making some changes within the basic framework. But if he really changes the way the world is apprehended . . . that's a much more radical move.

Q.: This is one of the perplexities of the self-referential language system, it seems to me. It sounds as though any connections it may have with external, sociopolitical reality call into question the artwork's integrity, its self sufficiency. Does the concept of a self-contained system limit the potential for confronting the world?

A.: No, I think we do it all the time. It's a question of how wisely we do it, how skeptically we do it, how playfully we do it. We can take the re-arrangement of consciousness that you get in Beckett and then suddenly see things in the world. Now that isn't what makes Beckett a great artist, but it's a consequence of great art. The world suddenly is what Beckett says it is in the play, and when you leave that play, the world is still a little bit what it is in the play. So what you've created is another model, a rich and wonderful model, and it does the job.

Q.: You've said that what keeps his characters alive is the flow of language, and his characters often become so obsessed with language it replaces the world. I think of Krapp luxuriating in the word, "spool"—it's far more real to him than the spool that sits in front of him on the table. That's potentially dangerous.

A.: Sure. Very. It's one of the topics of *The Tunnel*. It's a constant tension in art. That's why I have an historian in the novel. It is a very tempting doctrine to suppose that history is basically linguistic. That means that as soon as you remove that ultimate ground, you simply have power plays. This is why, although I'm very interested in alternative theory construction in philosophy, I would hold that there is in fact a reality that grounds our doctrines, and by which we can correct them. It's not just a kind of relativism between systems. I think that holds true for art, because artistic systems are not trying to make those statements. James was worried about this, although in the moral sphere. When you mistake artistic values for ethical ones . . .

Q.: Something like anti-Semitism can be awfully coherent.

A.: Indeed. And therefore immediately attractive.

Q.: It makes you as an artist very influential. It gives you political responsibility.

A.: Well, you have the same political responsibility as any citizen to keep from believing stupidities. To the degree that you want to promote political ideas in your work—as I say, the motives for writing are manifold, and it is not impossible to write beautifully *and* have a point of view—it seems very likely that you have to have responsible ones. That's why, for instance, I've never been very fond of Sartre, not only theoretically but personally, because I take him to be frivolous. With all that stuff about commitment, you look at his life—he really didn't do it. He had power and influence and used it frivolously. He adopted points of view that were dramatic and went from one silliness to another, what with having to support Stalin and then Mao . . . and that's irresponsible. A lot of the French intellectual tradition from Pascal on is infected with a kind of gamesmanship that I associate with *art*. I think it is one of the things Valéry saw very well, very clearly, and was one of the reasons he hated Pascal. You even see that point of view being carried on in criticism: adopting for certain areas a kind of play that involves rhetorical drama. I suppose as long as you do it in criticism it really doesn't matter; you say dumb things about Flaubert and people survive it. But if you then bring that out into the political arena and recommend behavior on the basis of the merely dramatic, it's immoral.

Q.: So you can manipulate your materials to fit your artwork, but if you try to carve up the world . . .

A.: That's Fascism. Fascism is attractive in part because there is so much of the tendency to treat the world as a work of art. That wonderful section in Burckhardt on the State as a work of art is very attractive in a way . . . until you see how horrible it is.

Q.: Two of the works that strike me as precursors to *The Tunnel* are *Notes from Underground* and Kafka's "The Burrow." I wonder if those are deliberate echoes in your novel.

A.: Actually, I hadn't even read "The Burrow" when I started *The Tunnel*, which of course has been in progress for a long time. I read *Notes from*

Underground as everybody does when he's a freshman, and I was never struck by it, although you never know how much those things percolate. Since I started the novel, of course, I've paid attention to it. But I think there's a great deal in my own background that would lead me in this direction. Then I began to pick up all the literary examples that go along with it. But I can remember back into my childhood enough about my kind of daydreams—the notions of tunnels were powerful images before much literary influence.

Q.: Burrowing in, forming barriers, creating a private space that can't be penetrated by ghosts—they're presumably common psychological tactics.

A.: Sure. And the ambiguity of it all denotes something common enough. I don't want it to be a "thin" notion, but I do think that the particular images that come to dominate a story have more significance for the writer than they would for the average person. Everybody has his own. And, of course, there are all kinds of tunnels. Now Kafka's burrows aren't tunnels exactly, because a tunnel is presumably going from A to B in order to get *through* barriers, to get beyond obstacles, to escape. But of course, in my book, the tunnel is itself the point. You're not going anywhere.

Q.: Your characters seem to lock the door only to find that they've closed themselves in with whatever they had hoped to escape from. I think of Furber trying to purge himself of his carnal urges. The purification rite is his obsession. Even though he doesn't commit the physical act. . . . One of the saddest moments in that book is when Furber makes love with the girl by imposing his shadow upon her.

A.: You can suffocate in your own fiction.

Q.: We've spoken before about the relative status in reality of historical and literary figures. Would you say that Huckleberry Finn is more "real" than, say, Alexander the Great because he is more fully realized in language?

A.: I certainly would. Not only that, but there are more people who lived with Huck as a real person—this may be a literary mistake, but never mind—and who see childhood, figures along the Mississippi, and the particular sociohistorical milieu in the United States in this way. Frequently the novelist creates the little people of the time. I'm working with that in this book. I'm pushing it, although the novel is not simply that. I don't think the purpose of the novel is to create important nobodies who stand as significant figures for their time. But that does happen, and it isn't all bad. If one understands Tom

Sawyer and Huck Finn well enough, then they are part of the American myth. They constitute important historical forces, and they are not divorced from all reality. Any viable myths of this sort have a grip on *something*. It's true of Faulkner. We don't even know yet how important it's going to be, when the Faulkner characters people our historical consciousness. Dickens did that—still does for a number of people, although his effect is no longer as dominant as it was.

Q.: In the *Partisan Review* interview, you said that poetry has grown careless, leaving fiction as "the advanced, hard and formal form." Would you elaborate on your disparagement of poetry? If you think of poetry, as many critics do, as the "purer" genre, it might be more conducive to the self-referentiality you seek.

A.: It would normally be, and this comes out of the Symbolist movement. One would associate it with Valéry or Mallarmé. It's just that at the present moment I think poetry is in a down phase, particularly in European literature. We passed through a phase of perhaps the greatest set of lyric poets we've had in European culture, and certainly the highest explosion of American poetic impulses. It's not unnatural that from Stevens we had lesser Lowells and Roethkes, and now we have less still. That I think is a temporary phenomenon. But it's also accompanied by the fact that there has been a great explosion, not of great poetry, but of poets. That hasn't helped matters. When you compare what is going on in poetry from the point of view of poetry in the larger, traditional sense, all the really fine poets now are writing fiction. I would stack up paragraphs of Hawkes, Coover, Elkin, or Gaddis against the better poets writing now. Just from the power of the poetic impulse itself, the "poets" wouldn't stand a chance.

Q.: It seems, too, as though poetry, especially free verse, is so open to spontaneity in a bad sense. And in the sixties, every performance was a work of art, and everyone was a poet, while the burden of significance was on the audience.

A.: It's easier to achieve a certain kind of pseudo-identity, too, by being a poet. . . . But I don't think poetry is anywhere near the stature of fiction now. The great figures will be back, but at present we have an extraordinary period of great novels.

Q.: So you're not one who worries about the continuing efficacy of the genre of the novel.

A.: All you have to do is look around the world and see what's being produced, the kinds of books that are coming out, the quality they have. Whether you're reading a new novel by Calvino or Vargas Llosa— sensational writers who write quite differently—or others still, who may write nothing like Hawkes or Barth . . . it's significant stuff that's coming out, it's important. When *JR* comes out, it's a monumental effort. And that kind of thing is happening all around—stunningly good stuff. I taught some contemporary novels last year in a philosophy and literature course— Fuentes's *Distant Relations* and Hawkes's *Virginie* were two of the books. None of them were the major works of their authors, all were different, yet all were first-rate. Fuentes was on the campus for about a month in April, and it was exhilarating to be around him, because along with so many of his compatriots, he's really revolutionizing writing. It's an exciting time.

Q.: The writers that you mention most often as personal favorites—Barth, Barthelme, Coover, Elkin, Hawkes, the South American "magical realists"— are these the contemporaries who can be most directly identified with your own literary theories?

A.: I would not expect, well, Fuentes to share my "hermeticism," I suppose. But when he was here—and I'm not sure why he did this—he made a point in his last lecture of referring to my views with approval maybe half a dozen times. Part of that may have been courtesy, but as I talked to him, and understanding his leftist leanings and so forth, his conception of what one had to do as a writer was very similar to mine. I think what has happened with a lot of writers—Fuentes, who started out on the Left, a realist, committed, as Calvino did—has been a shift away, a withdrawal of their radicalism, from parties. I also regard myself as a radical, but not one allied with any party. Parties force you to give up your intellect. I think we share an idea of things that need to be done, in a very general sort of way.

Q.: Is it possible to accomplish what needs to be done without those affiliations?

A.: I've never been called an "engaged" writer before. I don't have the deeply emotional commitment of a Márquez or a Fuentes. But both Márquez and Fuentes know that if they're going to have the social effect that they want to have, they're going to have to be artists first. Otherwise, their work won't be powerful enough, won't last long enough. It will get lost in the political climate. So they are much more susceptible to that contradiction. I felt it, of course, during the sixties, when we were out, marching and so on, but even then I had too much skepticism about all of this. Movements tend to falsify subtleties. Too often, the Sartrean idea is that we have to give this up because the end is so important, while you end up sacrificing the end as part of the means. I tend to be a Kantian about things like that. It does often throw you back into a position of increasing impotence. And that gets into my work. It's part of the reason that my work is as bitter as it is, I suppose. It's that sense of helplessness. You write essays on the Bomb, you go to conferences on nuclear holocaust—people think of me as a Holocaust expert now—and you get weary of that side of it. You have to be careful not to let the exasperation poison things. Perhaps I can get rid of it in a character.

Q.: You teach, or have taught, a course in philosophy and literature. Do you find that they work together easily, that they're compatible in the classroom?

A.: I use it to teach points of view that I don't share. Philosophy in literature is largely content analysis. But I find it fun to treat novels on the premise that they are constructing worlds, and that you can then ask what the philosophy of those worlds is—in the same way that you would ask it about *the* world—and see what goes on in the system to convey it. The structure, the plot.

Q.: Do you teach your own work?
A.: No.

Q.: If you were required to teach your own work, would you approach it as a diligent New Critic, so as to do the most justice to the language artifact? What method do you feel would show the fullest appreciation of what you try to accomplish in your work?

A.: I'm not sure. I think what you would have to do with my work, because of the attitudes behind it, is to pretend you were reading Montaigne. It's basically skeptical and uncommitted, so behind it are plenty of attitudes and values that are absolute, but in terms of the theoretical frame around them, they are held with a great deal of skepticism. I'd probably be inclined to do a New Critical approach because that's the way I was brought up, although that's not what I do in the class much. Mine is generally a philosophy class more than a literature class.

Q.: I wonder how you react to poststructuralist and other recent brands of criticism that assert themselves as works of art, rather than as something which is just occasioned by a work of art and is therefore of a second order of creation.

A.: Well, I think that is very interesting. It's been done in the past, and it can work, but the question is whether or not it is written well enough. I don't think most of it is. What you have is a clear move on the part of the critic to usurp part of the creative function *for* the critic. I have no objection to that. I understand it perfectly. I do it myself. But I wouldn't make it a critical premise. A lot of it is very interesting, but a lot of it cops out, attempting to earn for the critic a creative status on other bases than creativity. Generally, this critic is doing openly what critics have done for a long time covertly. Also, this type of critic wants to make the text malleable to his own manipulations, and that's just the opposite of what my aim is when I'm creating a text. I want a text to have levels and richness, but I want *it* to have that. My attitude toward the reader is one of creative passivity. When that critic approaches a text, he says that the reader is now in charge, in the sense that the text is raw material. What I believe is that when I'm reading, say Colette, the text doesn't become *me.* That's not what I'm reading her for. I want to become Colette.

Q.: Is that the most beneficial way of approaching a text? Joyce always talked about creating an ideal readership. And in *Willie Masters' Lonesome Wife,* if Babs is language herself, as lovers of language we are depicted as dilettantish, impatient, and not particularly skilled. Do you hope to create a readership by foisting demanding works upon them? In other words, do I learn how to read a Gass work by reading enough of Gass to become "schooled" effectively?

A.: It's a process of schooling. It is a process, too, of giving yourself to the work. The problem is that of removing yourself to the extent that you allow the work to interpenetrate your nature, your consciousness, rather than the other way around. If you don't have this point of view, then you cease to be as interested in quality, because you can make something out of anything, just as the artist may see something ugly and make it beautiful when he writes it up. The critic who says, "All the better if it's not very good in itself—it's much more easily disarmed," is not interested in the central problem as I see it, and that is the quality of the literary product. He's interested in texts, not in why one text is better than another. One of the reasons is that *he* is going to confer upon the text the value that it will receive. Even if Roland Barthes is going to develop a huge, complex process of decoding, he chooses a lousy story by Balzac.

Q.: It's as though the less successful work gives you more freedom to move around.

A.: And also, it's often simply more illustrative of what you are talking about. That was true of early Freudianism, too, which seemed to work best on cheap romances. Eventually, of course, you get a sophisticated Freudian doctrine. The same thing with Marxists: the early Marxist stuff worked best on junk. I think structuralists are still crude—you get some important insights, but everyone has his own little formulas which will be refined only eventually. It seems as though I've lived through many generations of formulas. When I grew up, it was all New Criticism, which sometimes was tiresome, but which did have something important to say.

Q.: It's still the primary approach in literature surveys, I think. It's one way of getting students to respect the complexity of literature proving it is accessible to formulas that are reminiscent of methods used in the sciences.

A.: And teachers foster the sense that it takes a special expertise to read literature adequately. It's one way of competing for respect these days.

Games of the Extremes: An Interview with William Gass

Jo Brans / 1984

From *Southwest Review*, (Autumn 1985), 438–50. Reprinted by permission.

"My fictions are, by and large, experimental constructions," William Gass has commented. "That is, I try to make things out of words the way a sculptor might make a statue out of stone. Readers will therefore find very little in the way of character or story in my stories." The most ardent of "art for art's sake" aestheticians, Gass, a writer, philosopher, and university professor, nevertheless reached a wide audience with his first novel and has maintained a steady readership with the two volumes of fiction and four volumes of essays he has published since.

Actually, in Gass's mind the distinctions between fiction and nonfiction have little credibility when applied to his work. "I think of myself as a writer of prose rather than a novelist, critic, or storyteller, and I am principally interested in the problems of style," he has said. And it is true that his essays are a lot closer to his fiction than they are to conventional nonfiction, and that both his fiction and his nonfiction sound like poetry.

Born in North Dakota in 1924 and brought up in Ohio, Gass decided at the age of eight or so to become a writer, and accordingly "read whatever came to hand," from detective stories and books about bees to biographies of Napoleon and *Thus Spake Zarathustra*. After three years in the Navy during World War II, he took a degree in philosophy in 1947 from Kenyon College, where he audited several classes of the Fugitive poet John Crowe Ransom. Ransom's New Criticism, a theory of aesthetics that stresses the independence of a literary text from any extra textual consideration, converged with Gass's own leanings toward formalism in writing.

From Kenyon, Gass went to graduate school in philosophy at Cornell, where he specialized in the philosophy of language and wrote a dissertation on "A Philosophical Investigation of Metaphor." "I love metaphor the way some people love junk food;" he has said. Receiving his doctorate in philosophy in 1954, Gass taught at Wooster College and at Purdue University. Since

96

1969, he has been a professor of philosophy at Washington University in St. Louis.

A high point of his years of graduate study at Cornell was a seminar conducted by the philosopher Ludwig Wittgenstein which Gass later described as "the most important intellectual experience" of his life. Wittgenstein views philosophy as an activity to be pursued for its own sake, apart from content. Another high was a growing familiarity with the work of Gertrude Stein. As Wittgenstein was interested in the process of philosophy rather than a fixed philosophical system, Stein was similarly interested in the process of writing, especially in the sound and significance of single words and repeated sentences, rather than the lifelike content of literature. From these influences and others, particularly the textual insularity of Ransom, Gass came to conceive of fiction as a construction made of metaphor, with no relevance to the world outside the book and no obligation to be "lifelike."

The central figure of *Omensetter's Luck* (1966), Gass's first and most conventional book of fiction, is the Reverend Jethro Furber, a "verber with fervor," a man whose whole life is lived in language. Set in conflict with Furber in the structure of the book is the almost silent Omensetter. The reader watches while Furber builds a structure made entirely of language, which has no counterpart in any reality except Furber's madly verbing mind, for the purpose of destroying Omensetter. Difficult though the book is, it was unanimously praised. "The fever is in the words on the page," one critic wrote.

In the Heart of the Heart of the Country (1968) is a collection of two novellas and three short stories. The title story has autobiographical elements, but Gass has insisted that the narrator, a poet "in retirement from love," has "a mind with severe limitations" and "a psyche whose feelings are full of self pity." Gass tries to get inside this character, as he tries to get inside the adolescent Jorge who is the narrator of "The Pedersen Kid," the longest story in the collection, and as he tries to do in his fiction generally. Both in *Heart* and in a second book of short stories, *The First Winter of My Married Life* (1979), Gass is more interested in the way his often damaged narrators tell the stories than in the content of the stories they tell. Because the concern of his work is with the process of its own creation, because his fiction takes itself as its own subject, critics have dubbed Gass a writer of "metafiction."

Willie Masters' Lonesome Wife (1971) has been called by the author an "essay-novella." The form of the story is an interior monologue of Babs, the wife, once a stripper and a whore, which takes place while she is having sex with a lover. A collage of divergent elements—authorial asides, little essays interspersed at random, parodies, footnotes—breaks up the narrative and makes for what Gass refers to as an experience in art. "You have fallen into art," *Willie Masters'* concludes, "—return to life."

On Being Blue: A Philosophical Inquiry (1976) is like a long Symbolist poem, in which every association with the word "blue" is explored through the use of image and metaphor. The "inquiry" concludes with an analysis of the blue, or sexual, content of literature, in which Gass theorizes that erotic fiction uses language "like a lover" to seduce the reader.

Gass has written three additional books of essays, *Fiction and the Figures of Life* (1970), *The World Within the Word* (1978), and *Habitations of the Word* (1985), in all of which he defends his theory that the artist has no obligations to morality or to life, but should content himself only with beauty of form and language. For *Habitations,* Gass received a National Book Critics Circle award. He has also received a Guggenheim Fellowship.

This interview took place on a rainy Sunday afternoon in Dallas in the fall of 1984. Gass is a round-faced man, with longish straight gray hair, and dark eyes. Exhilarated but surprised at the frankness with which he spoke of the loss of the *Omensetter* manuscript, I remember afterward running into the room where my husband sat reading, setting up the tape player, and demanding, "Put your book away. You've got to listen to this!"

Brans: I've been reading you a long time, you know—since *Omensetter's Luck* came out in 1966. I read you before I even knew you had a literary theory.

Gass: Good!

Brans: I wondered how you feel about being wedded to this theory, being known as the apostle of aestheticism.

Gass: People insist on it, but I don't think I really have a theory. A bunch of attitudes and opinions, maybe, but I've never written any general justification, any clear-cut, organized theory. I just take up little problems here and there, and anyway that's a separate activity.

Brans: From your writing fiction?

Gass: Yes, in the sense that I don't think about it when I'm writing fiction. I'm not interested in trying to write according to some doctrine. When I'm writing fiction, it's very intuitive, so that what happens, or what I do, or how it gets organized, is pretty much a process of discovery, not a process of using some doctrine that you can somehow fit everything into.

Brans: I'm relieved. I really loved *Omensetter's Luck,* but then I tried to fit your theory that art is nothing but form to the book, and it just didn't work. No matter how often your essays say that art and morality don't mix, I keep seeing morality, moral positions, in *Omensetter.*

Gass: A lot of people feel that way, but it doesn't bother me. I mean, I'm not concerned with it that much. I think partly it has to do simply with the connotations of a formalist position. But that's a mistake in understanding the word "formal." It's not formal in the sense of stripped or regular or anything of the sort. I am a romantic writer with a formalist theory. So that gives people problems.

Brans: And it gives you a lot of room too, doesn't it? Your great rival on the whole issue of art and morality for years was John Gardner, of course. I'm curious—were you and Gardner friends before he died?

Gass: Yes. We couldn't have been close because we never lived close enough to one another. But we were friends for a long time, first through correspondence. And then when he moved from California to southern Illinois, I visited him on his farm there. Then we saw each other more often when I was at Washington University. We were friends for about twenty-five or thirty years.

Brans: So the fact that you disagreed on this fairly vital subject didn't turn you off?

Gass: No, it didn't bother me. In fact, it was one of the bases of our friendship. We used to have wonderful arguments at three o'clock in the morning, in the kitchen over a bottle of bourbon. They were much better than the official arguments that took place.

Brans: Did you shout at each other?

Gass: Sure. But John was a very good-humored man, very kind and generous.

Brans: That wasn't a very good-humored book he wrote, *On Moral Fiction.*

Gass: No, it wasn't. People didn't get over it easily, either because they didn't know John well enough or didn't know the situation. John wrote that under difficult circumstances. Part of the time he was ill with cancer. Then part of it was written early, before he had published much. It was a kind of funny coming together of resentments when he was not well known and of the effects of this illness.

I think a lot of writers also felt that, since they weren't used to having John as a critic, he somehow turned on the writing group because he was attacking so many people, of such different sorts. I have found an enormous amount of dislike of John, even from writers who weren't mentioned who were mad because they weren't. So you can't win.

Brans: In interviews, I often ask writers where they place themselves in this controversy between you and Gardner—on the side of art for art's sake with you, or on the side of moral art with Gardner. John Cheever, for example, put himself on Gardner's side, as you would expect, but he wasn't too happy about having Gardner as his spokesman.

Gass: Most people, I would think, would lean in John's direction rather than in mine, but his book didn't help his cause. People didn't like its peevishness.

Brans: That's a good word. Well, how do you like having placed yourself against the attitudes of Cheever, say, and Saul Bellow and Iris Murdoch?

Gass: I feel very good about it, as a matter of fact. Though I admire those writers. They're very accomplished. I know Iris, and we've argued about this. I've never really discussed it with Bellow, but I admire his work very much—on my grounds.

Brans: You have some similarities. He has the same infatuation with language that you have.

Gass: Sure. And I don't care what position his book appears to espouse, or what the characters argue, as long as they fit into the book. What's disturbing to many of the writers like John is that they want something more than that. If I just keep what they want to say *in the book,* then I'm not allowing them to say it. But I just say, "All right, in *here,* that's what goes on."

The problem with the "moral" position comes when people start to theorize about it. Cheever, for example, had feelings of this sort, but he wouldn't erect a theory. Consequently, his attitude toward other writers could be very generous. Whereas, if you start erecting a theory, that theory then pretty soon is going to lead you into the Tolstoy problem. You're going to have to start kicking out too many people. And I don't have to do that. I can find formal value in a short story by John Cheever. I think that's why he's a good writer.

So I think that my theory, if you want to call it that, allows more people than the other one, so that's an advantage. I also don't, because of the kind of thing it is, take the theory so seriously. I mean, I don't, as I said before, approach reading somebody else's work with a doctrine in mind. I just read it, and I either like it or I don't like it. I'm either moved or I'm not. Then sometimes I have to find reasons. But most of the time I haven't bothered to do that. It would be a pretty sad life if you went around trying to figure out reasons why you like people—similarly for books, paintings, and so on. But when one is in that business, one is forced to do it.

Brans: I guess what bothers me about what I would call your extremism in, say, "Fiction and the Figures of Life," is that you imply that we are never changed by books.

Gass: Oh, we are changed, but not in any way the book could have foreseen. It isn't as if it is a cause and effect relationship. Here's an example I like to use: People are changed by other people. But the person that comes into other people's lives and changes them isn't like a hatchet falling; it is simply quite different each time, from person to person. Nor can a person who has that effect—well, it would be very odd if you had a child who was brought up to have a certain effect on everybody. Books have powerful effects certainly, we all know from experience, but the effects are very hard to measure.

I don't think of the effect so very much as a change of mind; sometimes books act as a kind of crystallization. You are ready to think a certain thing, or feel a certain way, or more in a certain way, and a book comes along and just does it for you. But by and large they become companions. They influence you because what is in them is incredibly valuable. But, again, not I think in the same sort of obvious way in which you fall in love with somebody and therefore take up all their opinions. That would be bad.

So I feel that although those changes are there, they are multiple and unpredictable, and certainly can't be traced to the author's intention or any specific thing. What's often a common denominator, whatever a book's opinion or attitudes, is that a book, because it's an example of excellence, may enshrine those attitudes. I can move from one writer to another and be moved by both, be changed by reading both. Then I look at the books and see they are quite different in every respect, including in their opinions.

Brans: To what extent are the heroes in your novels you?

Gass: Well, they're me in the sense that I think them up. They reflect some things of mine, but it's a mix. For example, the hero of *The Tunnel* is a not-nice person. He's a historian of the Nazi period, and he's got a lot of fascism in him. He doesn't go around murdering people; he's not wicked in that sense. But he's not good; there's a quality to his mind which I think isn't that of a hero. So I have to draw on a lot of things which are opposite to what I approve of—anti-Semitism, bigotries of other sorts. And if your book is going to have any dramatic power, you've got to give all the sides. Otherwise your book has no strength; it's just paper. Bellow is very good at this, maybe because he's an intellectual. He finds ideas powerful and he likes to get inside them, even if they are ideas he disagrees with.

Brans: This is true of you too.

Gass: I hope so, I hope so. It's partly the teaching business, where you get used to getting inside of another system of ideas and arguing it.

Brans: I remember a sentence in an essay you wrote, "Fiction is the ultimate act of voyeurism." That seems to be what you're talking about in writing about this man with the Nazi mind. But don't you feel fearful really? Somewhere else you say that the job of the writer is to take over the reader's consciousness. Suppose you really took over someone's consciousness with a powerful portrayal of this fascist.

Gass: But that indicts the reader. If a person accepts these things, then he is that sort of person in a way.

Brans: What do you mean?

Gass: I mean one of the strategies of the book is not to present this character as unattractive. We use this technique in philosophy too. You lead a student to an argument which seems innocent and as long as it seems innocent the student assents to it. And then he suddenly sees that all kinds of ideas which he holds must fall if he is going to accept this argument. You thus produce in the student the realization that he has been led into a trap.

I do this in the book a lot. I make the narrator attract you at certain times. Then you turn the corner and you see where that attraction leads. But if you were feeling the attraction, it must be that you have some of the same thing yourself.

Brans: You've been caught in the net. That's exciting!

Gass: Yes, I want the readers to find themselves saying, "Hmmmm," realizing that what they are assenting to is not benign.

Brans: Are you about finished with *The Tunnel*? I know you've been working on it for ten years or so.

Gass: Almost. There are lots of problems with it because it is visually, typographically, full of maneuvers which I hope won't be just gimmicks.

Brans: Like the things you did in *Willie Masters' Lonesome Wife*?
Gass: Even more of them.

Brans: I have to tell you I threw that book across the room. I had to go and pick it up and say, Well, okay, I'll do it. Then I liked it very much. But a book like that makes a demand of the reader.
Gass: *The Tunnel* won't be that hard at the beginning, but it's going to be a very demanding book. And it changes tone and style a great deal from section to section and even within sections. I can't imagine that most people will want to wade through it.

Brans: Then maybe no one will be tempted to steal the manuscript. Is it true that someone stole the only copy of the manuscript of *Omensetter's Luck*?
Gass: Yes, I was working on the last chapter—you know how short that chapter is—and had the manuscript on the desk in my office at Purdue. I went off to teach a class, and when I came back it was gone, just like that.

Brans: And you hadn't made any copies?
Gass: I had notes, but that was the only copy. My editor, afterward, kept insisting all the time, "Are you making copies? You send me material, *I'll* keep the copies."

Brans: But the thief couldn't have possibly brought the book out!
Gass: No, no, no, he tried to redo it as a play. That's how we learned who it was, though I had suspicions. I couldn't prove anything. Then he tried to change it around. He changed Omensetter to Hopewell, and he wrote this sort of play, and he showed it to some people who recognized it.

Brans: Did you prosecute?
Gass: No, the man left the country. He had done those things before, and gotten away with it.

Brans: You mean literally stolen other manuscripts?
Gass: Yes, from several people. He pretended he was putting together a collection of essays on [Nathanael] West, got someone to write a West piece, then stole it and published it under his own name. He had stolen something else from me in almost the same way. He told me he was collecting a volume of essays on Katherine Anne Porter for a publisher. And indeed I think this may have been a legitimate project at one time. He had written his disserta-

tion on her, knew her, showed her my manuscript—I have copies of their correspondence about it.

Then several years later, I happened upon an essay, and it was mine, almost word for word but not quite, under his name. Katherine Anne had complained about certain things I had said in the essay, and he changed a few things to soften it from her point of view, but that is about all he changed. The piece has been anthologized several times.

Brans: Was he certifiably loony?

Gass: Well, he was, I think, a very sick man. He was strange. He was very bright. He could be very personable. But he just had a compulsion—he was an orphan, if anything he ever told me was true.

Brans: I'm surprised you can keep from writing about this.

Gass: Well, I think I may be able to sometime, but my feelings were so strong at one time that I just couldn't manage anything. I mean, I couldn't talk about it even. Then one day six or seven years later I was driving down the street on the edge of the campus and I saw him on the sidewalk. I steered the car right at him—but it wasn't he. I stopped, and I was absolutely terrified and shaken, because I would have killed him.

Brans: You would have run right over him.

Gass: That's right. My feelings were that strong, and I suppose they still are. That unconscious hatred must be very great. It was a bad time.

Brans: Did anything good come out of that, do you think?

Gass: Yes, it did. I rewrote the book. Then I went to Urbana as a visiting teacher, and I put the book aside, feeling relieved that I'd been able to recover it. Several months later I got it out and looked at it, and I realized it was no good, I had to start all over again. That was the worst part. A whole lot of psychological energy went into facing that. It just seemed that I'd undergone this ordeal for nothing. Nevertheless it was good in the long run, because I got some distance, and I learned a lot from the whole experience.

Brans: That you might not have learned otherwise?

Gass: Maybe, or not so soon anyway. It just takes me a long time to get things right, if I'm going to get them right at all, and a lot of distance. That's one reason it's taken me so long to write *The Tunnel*. But everything is that way, even an essay. Rejections have almost invariably been an occasion for me to get very angry and furiously redo everything, and just as invariably there's an immense improvement, and I see it would have been really too bad if I had published the earlier version. Not that I'm giving the people who wouldn't print them any credit! I don't think that at all. But the delays, the impediments—

Brans: It would be bad for you to rush into print.

Gass: Yes. I've learned that. So now, if something doesn't happen, I make it happen. I slow things down.

Brans: What about a writer's connection between fiction and politics? I remember your addressing this in your review of Barthelme's *Unnatural Practices.*

Gass: I admired the work. It's very well done, and it's nice, and it's fun. His writing is very much socially oriented. There's a strong satiric, critical bent in everything he's doing. I probably feel just as strongly about what's going on in the country as he does, but I'm not an activist. During the sixties I was very active, but I was active because I was asked by people and sort of dragged into the situation. And even now, no one's less interested in literary politics than I am, and yet I'm in these meetings, I do a great deal. But once again it's being asked and feeling finally that you are obliged to say yes. Similarly I've done some speechmaking and written a few things on nuclear disarmament, but always at an invitation. But I'm not really an activist. I don't work in groups. I don't like groups.

Brans: Philosophers and writers usually don't, do they? Which matters most to you, philosophy or literature?

Gass: For me they're very similar. Philosophers create systems of ideas and relationships of meaning, very much as poets and novelists work. Philosophical systems are often to be valued as fictions, because very frequently they are quite hopelessly wrong. But they're still beautiful, and you can enter them, and you can see the world this way if you wish.

Brans: But you have to suspend disbelief.

Gass: Yes, but of course that's what one does when one reads a novel too. You work with that world, you accept its premises. But in philosophy the point comes when you say, "Yes, but is this so?" And then you treat it not as fiction, but as an alleged assertion about the world. Then come the fights and you start to poke holes in it and find it inadequate.

Brans: Philosophy is supposed to be a search for the truth and fiction isn't.

Gass: But in class, you see, you're not entirely just searching for truth.

You're trying to make clear to people what a certain system is and what it's like and why it goes the way it goes. Then while you're doing that, you're playing that you're in the system, you're following it. And that part of the teaching process is a literary one—you're playing with the system.

Brans: Just as you teach a novel by getting into it, no matter how extreme its characters are, and saying, "What's going on here? Why does he do this? Why does Gass make him do this?"

Gass: Sure, and while you're doing that, it's a similar activity. It's just that it works at a different level. In philosophy you're presumably talking about the world, but you're talking about it at a level of abstraction and law and generality, with very few concrete things—those are mainly the illustrations and usually misleading and bad ones. A novelist works with concrete things all the time, but the implications, the principles, are always there. So in that sense the two activities are very companionable.

There are, however, sharp differences. Coherence and rigor and clarity are good words in both fields, but they mean different things in each. A novel's aim is to be beautiful in this most general sense, and the aim of a philosophical system is to be true.

Brans: How can you not want to bring those two together though? Put the truth that you discovered in philosophy—

Gass: Because I think the philosophical theories that do that are wrong. I think that Plato was mistaken. Because he subordinates everything to the Good. There are some philosophers who don't, like Kant, who argues that the Good, the True, and the Beautiful, if you use the old trinity, are very distinct things. Now they can *appear* together, be intermixed in objects, that's certainly true, but they're different qualities, differently determined. I am convinced of that. That's one of the places of course where I argued with John.

Brans: And with Iris Murdoch. She has a phrase, "the corruption of philosophy." She argues that philosophy *keeps* us from knowing right from wrong.

Gass: Yes, she wants to say that with philosophy we've banished good and evil, and she wants to make those metaphysical categories again. Which is another philosophical enterprise, of course, though it's not the prevailing mode. And again, she's wrong, but it works wonderfully for fiction. She should think that way. Her fiction's wonderful.

Brans: What is "good" for you? What is the greatest good?

Gass: I really don't think there is one. I'm mostly skeptical about philosophical issues.

Brans: Not human kindness, not the act of writing, not creativity?

Gass: I think those are good, but I don't think there is such a thing as the greatest good. There are arguments in Kant that good will is the only unqualifiedly good thing.

Brans: Is that love?

Gass: No. It means being ready to subordinate your intentions to the categorical imperative, which is really a notion of treating everyone as an end in himself. I have some difficulties with that because it's hard to make clear what's involved, but no one should ever be treated as a mere means. That leads to a hatred of all kinds of coercion. I certainly have that. I don't even give to the United Way, because I feel it's a coercive solicitation and not a free one.

But freedom from coercion is only one of the good things. There's Aristotle's self-realization, to realize your essential capacities and so on. But I wouldn't want to do what Aristotle does, say "This is it!" Because all these things are important. Utilitarians are quite wrong about most things, but I do think that human society should be dedicated to the maximizing of freedom not the greatest happiness for the greatest number, but the greatest freedom for the greatest number of people.

But all this is an ordinary way of looking at things: to speak about moral values in terms of the intrinsic value of the individual, political values in terms of freedom, and personal, values in terms of Aristotelian realization. It's just not very exciting.

Brans: So it's more fun to write about the guy in *The Tunnel*?

Gass: Of course, to get out to the edge of experience. I love to play the games of the extremes, but when it comes to the actual, I recognize all the problems, and I don't want to be anything like that.

Brans: Why is sex your central metaphor? Or would you agree that it is?

Gass: It's not sex, it's the language of sex. That is, there's very little sexuality in my work, but there are a lot of sexual words. I have very few steamy sexual scenes, if any. The metaphor is fundamental, sure. But my interest in that subject and my use of a character's sexuality are almost invariably either symptomatic or metaphorical, whereas for a great number of writers sex is the direct subject.

Brans: Symptomatic?

Gass: Yes, symptomatic of some larger quality in the character that isn't directly sexual at all—dominance, power, or what might be called the verbal sexualization of the mind.

Brans: Wait a minute, let me run that by again.

Gass: It's the sort of thing you get in a character like Jethro Furber when the language becomes so eroticized that—

Brans: Oh, yes, he's making love with words.

Gass: Yes, and everything that comes into him falls into a nest of images that transforms it in that way.

Brans: But you could have used another set of—

Gass: Oh, I could have. Well, no, I don't think I could have, because I certainly think that, with respect to creativity, the sexual images are basic.

Brans: I'm being very fancy, but I wondered if your using them had something to do with the generation of the fictional world.

Gass: It's basic, but again it always operates at a symbolic metaphorical level.

Brans: I'm not really accusing you of having a dirty mind or anything like that.

Gass: Oh, I do have. However, on the whole, it's not the direct object of my interest. It's light I will throw on that object that's a sexual light. I think it has to do with my conviction that language becomes the object it displaces not just for sexual impulses, but for everything.

Brans: So that everything can be experienced in language.

Gass: What happens for a writer frequently is that what you can't control in the world becomes moved on to the page where you can. And not only control but express: things you couldn't express in the world you can express on the page. Or you can try out, so that the words then become more real than their objects.

Brans: Which is what happens to Furber; he completely forgets that Omensetter is a real person, and he has to be recalled to that at the end.

Gass: That's right. That happens with my characters all the time.

Brans: There's a sort of androgyny in one of your stories, "The Order of Insects." That's a really wonderful story. Is what this woman, this narrator, sees in the roaches the order that you see through your stories? She has the artist's mentality?

Gass: Yes, sure, she's seeing the world as an artist, trapped in a world which does not allow her to have that kind of consciousness.

Brans: She's not supposed to think that roaches are beautiful. They're the enemy of the housewife.

Gass: So the moment you do, you have stepped quite outside the whole role, of course. That's the sign. It's not a feminist piece, I guess.

Brans: It's so close to what Sylvia Plath does in her work—I'm thinking of her as the archetypal contemporary female writer. It really is an act of voyeurism that you can see the contradictions of the two roles of housewife and artist.

Gass: Well, one feels that it isn't hard to put yourself in that kind of role, because in a sense you are in that kind of role yourself.

Brans: Who's this "you"?

Gass: Most people. One of the great enemies of an artistic life is distraction—the impediments of every day, standard responses, and all the rest. Everybody has them. It doesn't matter what you're doing.

Brans: So that for her to make an unstandardized response like seeing the roaches as beautiful . . . But they're dead! If you could only see the live roaches.

Gass: No, they're always dead.

Brans: So they're only beautiful to her when they're dead. That's chilling. Is art full of dead roaches?

Gass: It's only when . . . It's hard to inspect a roach when it's alive.

Brans: What do you mean when you end *On Being Blue* by saying it's for all those people who live in the country of the blue? Who lives there?

Gass: It's the James story ["The Next Time"]. It's not a terribly good story, but I like the moral of it.

Brans: Now there you are, you see! You even talk about the morality of fiction!

Gass: But it isn't a terribly good story. It's about a man who decides to write a popular success. And he fails, and it's a masterpiece. He says, Oh, well, the next time I'll really get a winner. And he fails again, of course—it's just another wonderful book.

And so at the end he resigns himself and says, All right, I'll just have to live in the country of the blue. That's the realm of the purified and uncorrupted imagination, not the commercial. So my book is in a sense addressed to all of those who live in that place.

William H. Gass in Germany

Heide Ziegler / 1995

From *Anglistik,* 7.1 (1996), 69–75. Reprinted by permission of the author.

In August 1995, Gass taught a seminar entitled "The Medium of the Imagination" within the series of the "Stuttgart Seminars in Cultural Studies," which have taken place regularly at the Monrepos Castle Hotel in Ludwigsburg near Stuttgard since 1993. These seminars seek to promote cultural understanding between Europe and the United States and to provide a forum for multicultural, interdisciplinary dialogue. The interview with William H. Gass (W.H.G.) was conducted by Professor Heide Ziegler (H.Z.), who presently serves as the Rector of Stuttgart University, at Monrepos on August 15, 1995. Her review essay on Gass's new novel *The Tunnel* was read in the section on Modern American Literature at the Copenhagen Conference of the International Association of University Professors of English (IAUPE) on August 1, 1995. R.A.

H.Z.: Your long-awaited novel, *The Tunnel,* finally appeared in February 1995. Sections from this book were published in various journals over the last twenty-six years, and they differed so much in tone and mood that the reader did not know what to expect from the novel as a whole. On first looking at the tome as it has now been published, what immediately strikes the reader is that in *The Tunnel* you seem to fuse various arts. Music: the book has twelve sections relating to Schönberg's chromatic scale; painting: there are black and white or colored images—pennants, comics, etc. There are also various kinds of typography which draw attention to the Gutenberg art itself. You said that you are very serious about these various devices; why?

W.H.G.: Well, for lots of reasons, I guess. One is that I wanted to make sure that the text which the narrator is engaged in creating is as personal, odd, and as far from the historical research and writing he has been doing as possible. You don't find cartoons, doodles, limericks, and so on, in any ordinary history book. I wanted to convince the reader that the text he or she is reading is an entirely private one; that it has no ultimate or public aim. How better to do that than crumple a page? Draw faces? Muck about? I also wanted

sonic visual reinforcement for the doggerel, and to illustrate the kinds of
incursion into the text of the various voices which make up the narrator's
complex nature. Some of these designs are visual corollaries for the limericks
and other sorts of verbal play. I also wanted to return the text—in a crude
way—to the kind of illustrated books we saw the other day in the *Landes-
bibliothek* . . . those illuminated manuscripts. In one sense they "illuminate."
In another, they obfuscate, for certain things must appear in this manuscript
that are forever unexplained. These manipulations are evidences, evidences
of a mind operating very oddly, and they also personalize the text in a way
that the narrator couldn't merely by means of language, because in normal
books the type is always the same in every copy. I wanted the paper to
become personal. The drawings needed to be light, dashed off. They couldn't
look professional. They had to be like Kohler's signature, and reflect his
hand. Type is mechanically produced and no more individual than a nail.
Anyway, I've always been very interested in the relationship between the
visual and the auditory elements of a text. The auditory can be performed by
the reader, that is, the reader hears the words in the head, whereas the visual
is just there, presented to the reader like pie on a plate. The tension in the
word between sound and shape, and then again, between these material elements and the concepts in the mind and their referents in the world, has been
a constant concern in my work. From the publisher's point of view, the auditory aspect is cheap because it is automatically present in the print and the
reader is expected to play its music; whereas the visual aspect has to be
exemplified in the text in all sorts of ways. Not that the visual isn't there, but
the reader is used to ignoring it. If you adopt a symbolism of variable spacing,
or of typeface change—devices of that sort—not to mention colored pennants, armband designs, and so on, you are costing the publisher money,
because it takes a lot more money to print in color. To put into the visual side
of the text as much complexity and interest and continuity as is going into
the auditory side would have made the book far too unwieldy and far too
expensive, and probably not very wise, because it would have been a kind of
overkill. I had to back off from many of my original plans. Many of these
antics were visual puns, designs which reflected (as I did in *Willie Masters'
Lonesome Wife*) the very great ontological distance between the conceptual
and the actual: text written on a grocery sack, for instance, which represents
a sack of oranges Kohler and his mistress once shared together, the sack they
shared making love, and the sack she eventually gave him, when her love was
what . . . ? . . . lorn . . . lost. If the narrator begins to write on such a bag,

what does it tell you about him? Many of the results I wanted were impossible to achieve because I simply couldn't make each page physical enough, or suggest sufficiently this book's basically unbound unbooklike character. By crumpling a page and allowing other pages to weigh it down and flatten it again, I would have been able to suggest the weight and number of those pages, the weight of the life they relate. However such ideas had to remain notional. Perhaps the reader can still "get the idea," but getting the idea is not the same as feeling the effect.

H.Z.: You wanted it to be unbound from the first, no?

W.H.G.: Yes, I did. I knew I would never get my way, and that such a format was impractical, but conceptually that's what I wanted.

H.Z.: You have never really worked within a particular genre; in fact, you seem not to believe in genres. Is that the reason why you call *The Tunnel* an anti-novel?

W.H.G.: Well, I do believe in genres, but I believe in them because their rules and regulations can be occasionally violated with some significance. The crack in the Golden Bowl carries a powerful meaning. Before the crack, however, there must be both the gold and the bowl. I had the partisan desire to write a book which would undermine the ordinary organizational principles of fiction, not that what I've actually done is very original—it's not—but I like to take a lot of the conventions which are found in other fictions and cram them all together like commuters at rush, pushing them to the limit. Traditional historical narratives are orderly and clear and as linear as string. They are also utterly unlike life. My book is meant to be the inside of narrative, its pulp and seeds, not the rind. It is intended to undercut history, not only by misusing narrative techniques in general, but by revealing the mind of the historian, the life of the historian who has written this history (*Guilt and Innocence in Hitler's Germany*) and employed these modes. *The Tunnel* makes the life of the historian public. It's his official history which is hidden.

H.Z.: If your novel is not, as one reviewer stated, "modernism's last gasp"—is it postmodern?

W.H.G.: I don't think so, but then I've never been clear about the nature of postmodernism in literature. I think a lot of people would call the book postmodern because of the use of visuals, the presence of certain kinds of epistemological difficulties, and my extensive use of quotation, but all those things have been done before. I think of my work as late or decayed mod-

ern—yes, last gasp will do—but it may be that postmodernism is simply a
foregrounding of techniques and approaches which were found more in the
background in the past, then certainly it is postmodern. It just depends by
what you mean by this slippery term which makes sense to me only in an
architectural context, and there signifies a rather shallow historical eclecticism. I do say that in this novel, qualities which were once marginal for
fiction are made central, and things which were formerly central are thrust
toward the edge.

H.Z.: [This certainly seems to be true with regard to your treatment of
"setting."] Your narrator, William Frederick Kohler, allegedly spent some
time in Germany in his youth. Yet, in this novel, Germany seems to be a
landscape of the mind, not a true landscape, whereas the American midwest
is certainly made to appear "real"—with its duststorms, grasshopper plagues,
etc. Is this difference significant?

W.H.G.: Yes, because the book isn't really about Germany; it isn't really
about the Holocaust; it isn't about the narrator's historical work either. There
has to be enough of Germany (Holocaust and History) in it so that Kohler's
contact with that world is both specified and specific. However, the book is
basically about the midwest. It is basically about life in the United States,
about States of Disunity in soul and mind. Nothing else is treated in detail.
No, to do that I would have had to change the nature of the book and I would
have had to do a lot of research which I wasn't interested in doing and had
not time for. I've read a lot about the Holocaust and Nazi Germany out of
ordinary interest, but never did any note taking on these affairs. There are a
couple of moments in the novel where particular details are employed—
certain aspects of *Kristallnacht* are described, for instance—still, by and
large, Germany is as far in the background as a low range of distant hills.

H.Z.: Yet Kohler is an historian, and we meet a number of his colleagues
from the history department: Culp, Planmantee, Herschel, Governali. However, if, as you seem to suggest, these colleagues are just facets of the narrator's mind, do you mean to imply that all historical points of view are
relative?

W.H.G.: I want to leave that matter basically undecidable . . . not unde-
cided, undecidable: are these "real" people in the "real" world, and to what
degree, if it comes to that? To what extent—if they are "realities"—is their
character colored by Kohler's nature, because he is the one who presents
them to us? It is perfectly possible for a person to exist in the world, and be

described by somebody else, or looked at and interpreted by somebody else, in such a way that they become simply a reflection of the person doing the describing. I wanted to leave the ontological status of these characters in doubt. Either these are real people in his world, whom he, however, sees in this or that specific way, which is as much a reflection of his nature as theirs, or they are simply aspects of his own personality mildly at war with one another. People are, in my view, many people. It's not that we fall apart all the time into separate personalities, but under certain circumstances we display different values and feelings and modes of thinking. Kohler is, in some ways, at once a hard-boiled positivist (like Planmantee), and an operatic romantic (like Governali). Herschel represents Kohler's underlying decency—I hope it's there—while Culp is the mocker, and the side of him which cannot allow anything to become profound or serious, and who lowers life to the level of the limerick, the joke, the cartoon. I tried to give each of these characters a little bit of life, a little bit of independence. Each represents a theory of history, and each gets his own little story. That way I can also implicate Kohler in the history of his own time, to which he seems largely oblivious or indifferent, because he can be simultaneously a sneering outsider and a disastrously decimated person, a raptur(ed) romantic and a sweetly passive observer.

H.Z.: How do you account for the excellent literary taste of your narrator? His taste in many an instance, seems to resemble your own literary taste, and many reviewers have taken you up on the similarity. How did your narrator develop that taste and how does it relate to his view that history, all events, are, in the final analysis, shit?

W.H.G.: Kohler does share many of my "literary" preferences, but the reviewers tended to identify me with my narrator on more obvious grounds, I think (name, rolypoly body, etc.). However, Kohler does not have my taste in the sense that he doesn't interpret texts or esthetic objects the way I do. He doesn't give literature any independence. Every book or poem is Kohler magnified, reflected, manifested. There are also certain writers whom he values for qualities I would not esteem. I love Hardy as a poet, but I don't care for his novels much, for instance. The problem I had was complex. I had to create a character who possessed quite sophisticated attitudes and perceptions, not only toward literature but to culture in general. Yet that character had to retain all his more vulgar and mean-spirited traits as well. The "higher cultural qualities" he has do not ultimately keep him from holding views which are morally horrific. This paradox repeats itself in German history. It is a paradox which is central to the structure and the themes of the novel. If I had tried to make Kohler's taste quite a good deal different from mine, I would have had, first of all, to construct a sensibility from "another era." I would want it to be sophisticated, and I would want readers to recognize it as discriminating, but it could only be (if not mine) too predictably German. The resemblances between myself and my narrator are wholly trivial, I think, but I did emphasize them in order to test the reader's sophistication (a test many reviewers failed). Though the common reader takes shelter in autobiography as if from rain, the identification they should make, and what the book suggests, is with the narrator and his narrowness and spite. Kohler is not just an odd individual whom one can dismiss as a freak and a monster. Kohlers make up much of what mankind is. So, if I'm going to say this, then I also have to be there, close at hand, to establish the connection. How can I ask the reader to make such an unpleasant inference, if I haven't preceded him? Then part of this problem was a technical one. I did want to use some aspects of my own childhood which I felt were appropriate to my theme, so I did borrow a bit from my family history, though I distorted and minimized and skewed it. It also helped me to work near the edge of myself with respect to my character—a risky business all round, and I have paid some price for this closeness. Unfriendly reviewers delight in the opportunity to clothe me in Kohler's rags. However, the record will show, I believe, that I do not belong in Kohler's camp. Conservatives hate the book because it is a portrait of them. In the family of man there they sit.

H.Z.: Is it true that the second son of the narrator is named Adolph? Or is he supposed to be nameless? The prototypical brat? Why is the narrator, whose childhood is so important to the meaning of the novel, not made to relate to his children—not even in a negative way?

W.H.G.: The implication is clear enough, however the kid's name is never named. Therefore the child has an implied name but not a name. Lots of things in this book remain mysterious (like life). Kohler's relationship to his own parents considerably defines his attitude towards children. From his behavior toward them we can infer something about his unwillingness to have children in the first place, and his annoyance with his fatherly state. They aren't any great shakes, either, which we must imagine injures his ego. Moreover, they are clearly in Martha's care, and her kids, not his. How this came about can only be inferred from their relation and its deterioration over time.

The text implies that Kohler's wife named his first kid Adolf out of spite. Now the reader is welcome to consider the likelihood of this. Clearly Kohler doesn't want to think about him. So he doesn't. He is a person who shoves everybody into a realm of the lifeless. Kohler hates families. That is something interestingly unGerman about him. The contemporary world in general has been compartmentalized. His wife—he sees as little of her as possible— his kids the same. Who does he pal around with? He was close to his mistress, Lou, long ago. Now, no one. People who have had an unpleasant childhood often don't want to pass injury on, either. Who wants to play father when father has been a right wing meanie? The key passage for the handling of this theme is "Child Abuse." There Kohler has some of the feelings most parents have at one time or other, driven to distraction; still he does less, expresses less cruelty, than many who injure their children. It's never what he *does* which defines him, only what he *thinks,* or what he *refuses to think.*

H.Z.: Did the mind of the narrator undergo a development during the twenty-six years you spent writing the novel?

W.H.G.: I wouldn't say his mind underwent any change, though it took me a while to decide what kind of mind I was dealing with. In the early years of the book's formulation there may have been changes. I wouldn't call it development. I'd call it a process of constructing the character. In the novel itself there is a change, a change of feeling, I think, but it's not so much a change of mind. The narrator moves steadily into the past as the novel proceeds, and there is an increasing sensitivity to what he remembers. Better sides of him show up, particularly his sympathy with his mother's plight. The book begins biliously, but moves into other regions with his relation to his old professor, Magus Tabor, with his love for Lou, his recollections of his mother, and so on. The past becomes more complete, is more real than the present.

H.Z.: And yet is the past not also the source of what you call the fascism of the heart? This fascism of the heart seems to be a common human feature. Or are some people exempt from it? How does this fascism relate to the political ideology called fascism?

W.H.G.: Fascism is a tyranny which enshrines the values of the lower middle class, even though the lower middle class doesn't get to rule. It just gets to feel satisfied that the world is well run. It likes symbols of authority and it likes to dress up. It likes patriotic parades. It believes in "family values," that is the woman in the kitchen, the kids in kindergarten, and dad in the driver's seat. It likes to abolish day to day history by being excessively neat and tidy. It hates anything alien, strange, new. It bows [to], if it does not worship, authority. It is permanently resentful of its lower middle class position. And if any member leaves for wealthier regions, you can count on them behaving like one of the nouveau riche. However, readers who move from the fascism of the heart to form the analogous political condition, will make a mistake in my opinion. Kohler's mind goes astray because his feelings go astray. In the soul (not the mind) . . . in the soul fascism is the domination of passive emotions over active ones. I mean passive emotions in Spinoza's sense. That's why I began the book with the banners representing these feelings. My book is another book about human bondage. Political fascism is physically brutal. The fascism of the heart is a corrupt state of feeling, a realm of impotent resentment. In political fascism, the petty is perfected, the small boy struts his stuff, the bully has the run of the yard. In the fascism of the heart we hear the music of the aggrieved, the peevish, the spiteful-the concert of the coward.

H.Z.: What, by the way, are your next projects?

W.H.G.: *The Tunnel* functioned as an avoidance book. Its unpleasant presence made me write other books in order to avoid writing it. I have the bad habit—a passive emotion again—of fleeing one project as soon as it becomes difficult, justifying my flight by turning my energies to something else of sufficient importance that I can calm my conscience, and avoiding the horror of writer's block. As a consequence about five books came to the same stages of completion over a long period of time. I was finally able to break through with *The Tunnel* and get it out of the way. The next book, a collection of essays called *Containers of Consciousness* is already at the publisher's, and will be coming out next year. Then there is a work on the relation of architectural form to literary form which is nearly finished. It needs a bit more polish. It's actually another collection of essays, but these essays are formed around the architecture of literature. Borges' "Library of Babel" plays a part, so does Calvino's invisible cities. But the principal piece is on the spatialization of grammar and syntax, as well as the other formal elements which make sentences interesting. I am concerned in this book, with problems of notation. Following that is my book of photography. Again, it will be about the nature of form, visual form this time, using twelve of my photographs (the number may vary), and then writing about the esthetic issues they pose, and, I hope, help resolve. Once people define you in terms of your vocation, anything else you do seems a hobby to them. So I'm trying to be taken seriously mounting shows and so on. Unfortunately for my character, I don't have hobbies. The last project hanging on from the past is a little book *On Reading Rilke* which will require me to finish my "translations" of the *Duino Elegies,* now nearly complete. I regard my translations as "readings," and I shall be exploring translation problems, as well as Rilke's esthetic and the "meaning" of this great series of poems. After the past has been laid to rest, I should like to return to my real love, the novella. I think that is what I should have been doing all along, writing storyless stories.

A Talk with William H. Gass

Idiko Kaposi / 1995

From *Hungarian Journal of English and American Studies*, 3.1 (1997), 3–18. Copyright © by HJEAS. Reprinted by permission. All rights to reproduction in any form are reserved.

Q: Both as a reader and as a professor, you have a reputation of preferring European and Latin-American literature. Is this because you don't find enough challenge or pleasure in American fiction in its present state?

Gass: Well, not entirely. I've been interested in European literature since I was a kid for some reason. Instead of being particularly attracted to English novels for example, I was attracted more to German and French and even Italian. So that's been a sort of fixation since I was very young. When I was in high school. I was reading Thomas Mann, and the combination of philosophical interest with Mann was very attractive. Then the French novel particularly became fundamental. But I continue that interest in part because in courses I teach here, it's simply an opportunity for me to introduce American students to literature they never see, hear about, or read. They're so caught up in the English language. But it's also true that the scene is wider. I mean in the United States we have some very interesting writers indeed but they just multiply present possibilities. And then for a long time the novel's impetus as a new form (or developing form I should say) has been in the hands of a few Europeans, Calvino or Bernhardt, or in Latin-America. Since that Latin-American tradition is now slowing down, it shifted the Spanish language to Spain. You have all of that intense experimentation, but France for example right now is pretty slow. It varies, it just changes. The US in the '60s was very exciting, as well as everywhere else.

Q: From an alien perspective, the whole contemporary American scene seems to be overtly politicised. The new schools of interpretation, whether they take on postcolonialism, gender issues, or black aesthetics look at literature from a very political point of view. Do you agree with this?

Gass: Yes, that's true. That's because the US's literature in the past has not been highly politicised, because it simply wasn't intellectual enough. And now it's not any more intellectual, but the politics is not a politics of theory about the best political system to have, it's about getting yours. Each group wants their part of the pie. It's a different kind of political manoeuvring than "workers of the world unite." And it's provincial, and it's political only in terms of the slice of the power. We see a lot of that both in gender differences, race differences, and in minority groups as well. Then you add to that a theoretical picture which suits each interest. So you get some very strong things; some of the best writing being done in the country is coming from Asian-Americans, Latinos, etc., the younger people. Some of the older honky types are just boring and not doing much. When the political stuff passes, as I think it will eventually, we'll have the same thing happening that has always happened to American literature: we'll be reenergized by immigration. New groups come in, they tend to go through similar kinds of work. They write about how it is to grow up in the slums, that sort of thing, over and over. But they have the new energy as always. So we'll get its advantages again. Furthermore now we don't just have a black writer here or there, we've got lots of very good ones, and the good ones are less and less political by the way—it's interesting.

Q: Politics seems to affect not so much the writers as the different schools of criticism.

Gass: Yes, that's true. Each theory has been perfected for each kind of political movement. But it's not good for the writers to be captured by a movement. They want to capture writers, they want them to do things, but they still lack—as deconstruction I think basically does—a firm intellectual ground. They speak like dolls: "We want! We want!"

Q: You're indeed famous for being anti-deconstructionist. Though now deconstruction is largely over, or at least the exclusiveness they had is gone.

Gass: Yes, pretty much. And here at Wash U it was never strong. That's partly to our merit, but mostly it's just by default. We didn't have a strong criticism group here at the English department or elsewhere; our critics were much more historical. Deconstruction never got going very much here. I've visited other universities—it's amazing how powerful and active and crazy it was in other places.

Q: What do you think comes next?

Gass: I don't really care. I don't think political or literary critical fads amount to much. They occupy graduate students, but that's good. I mean graduate students should be excited about new things, get freshly involved. Theories just pass and sometimes they leave some decent residue, but the

best literary criticism has always been done by writers. There's hardly anybody of lasting character in criticism who isn't a writer, and a good one, too.

Q: Can we go as far as also to suggest that the frustrated writer makes the
critic?

Gass: Not necessarily. I think a lot of critics are interested basically in
politics or ideas of that sort, but they are not either good enough or not
concerned enough to pursue the discipline of philosophy or political science.
So literature becomes a soft subject with which you can do psychology, you
can do history, philosophy, all these others without really doing history or
psychology. And this allows them to avoid doing literature, which is rather
hard. Among most literary or language departments you encounter the problem of people who really don't like literature as literature very much.

Q: A critic once wrote that your ideal is "the ultimately self-enclosed,
self-referential world of words." It would be difficult to hold this quote up
against you, first because it would be impossible to break out from the barriers of the language you were born into, your mother world of words, and also
because some of your works, especially *The Tunnel,* do reach out from the
realm of art and words, taking on the issue of the Holocaust.

Gass: Well, that position has been frequently misunderstood, almost invariably. The view I have is not that works of literature shouldn't have ethical-political interests. It's impossible to exclude them, it's sort of crazy to.
But I believe that the judgment of the ethical excellence of the work depends
on formal conditions. That doesn't mean that lots of the material being used
in a book—its themes or subjects—are not meant to be about anything at all,
including of course political subjects and all sorts of other things. Ethical,
political, and social concerns will be present in every writer's work at every
point. The question is not that; the question is how you write about them. For
me, it is perfectly reasonable to judge a work of literature as if it were a work
of persuasion and say I approve of that or I don't; then you're not talking
about its aesthetic qualities, that's all. My position is to try to separate aesthetic qualities in terms of judgment. Of course they're going to be all mixed
together, but in terms of judgment the truth, the good, and the beautiful are
separate values, found always together but judged differently. My view is
that you don't judge a work to be beautiful because it's morally uplifting or
tells the truth about things. And it's perfectly possible for a work to be beautiful and not tell the truth, and in fact to be morally not a very nice thing.
Ideally of course it would be all these things at once. Why not. This notion

of self-referentiality is that literature is aesthetically to be judged in internal conditions. that's all.

Q: Do you believe that the work that is aesthetically perfectly put together supersedes the piece of reality it was written about?

Gass: Well, this philosophically in fact happens. And that's because texts do have a different kind of reality than the events they describe. It's not the fault of anybody or anything, it's just that texts do have universal elements, and they repeat, and they have an opportunity to occur in many many minds, whereas ordinary events do not. Ordinary events will be lost; their existence as facts, their meaning, their significance will be lost if they're not reported. There's nothing political about this, as if you were trying to get texts to take over. They just happen to have that kind of reality. And they last, just the way an institution tends to last longer than the individuals who participate in it. That's the way those things are structured. Texts last longer generally, they can have more effect over a longer period of time. Photographs, other works of art often do the same thing. They are often the only record we have of something that historically comes and goes.

Q: There has been a lot of talk about a recent cultural shift, the emergence of the electronic culture, the post-alphabetic era. Do you see this change, and how do you think it affects fiction?

Gass: Well, it's kind of hard to guess that. And the reason for being fairly sure we're going to get it wrong is that we have had, even in my lifetime, an enormous series of technological changes that have changed really the whole way the world works. And most of these have been media things, but not entirely. As everyone knows, the invention of the elevator created the possibilities of high rises. The automobile has just an incredibly important ad evil influence. And one can't predict the consequences when the car gets invented and people start to motor around little country roads in it, or what it's going ultimately to do, or things that it's going to affect, or that what it does will be positive or negative. It will be positive for some and negative for others; some very complicated results will follow. Now, we get all of this new technology, and it's really difficult to be sure. It used to be said that photography was going to replace painting. But what photography did ultimately was to liberate painting, so that it didn't have to do lots of the things that photography was able to do. What became a problem was that the photographers, or many of them, became no longer interested in doing reality picturing, and they had to free themselves of that task in order to create works of art. You never know what's going to happen. And people say, well, the electronic age is going to change the world. It's certainly going to make changes, and it's certainly opening up all kinds of possibilities. And human beings tend to be the kind of people who have to realize these possibilities, although every possibility isn't necessarily a desirable one. And that is taking place at the same time as genetic engineering opens up others—there are just a number of enormous possibilities. But the fact is that language is still going to remain the key thing, I think, for three fundamental reasons. Before we get to the machinery, before we get to any of these other things, we have to learn the language, both speaking and writing. And these are keys not simply to manipulating, but to thinking. Human communication in a direct way is basically verbal. Your own conscious life is carried on basically, in words rather than images. Some, of course, is imagery, but basically it is language. And I see no replacement for that in technology. Possible enrichment, possible ease in doing things, possible weakness too of people not getting a good linguistic grip on things. But the question of whether the book as an object survives is I think less important. I have no question about whether language will. It's still the basic key to everything, and the technology really increases its importance. We may organize it differently, we may make our connections in a more radically different way. The sign systems, even if we go to a visual sign system, have to be read and interpreted on the basis of linguistic models. As for what other things will emerge . . . People have a vested interest in technology, and are lead by their enthusiasms to make extreme claims: "We don't need that now, we have this." But the fact is that high-powered computers were made possible by symbolic logicians, and are run on language's syntactical principles.

Q: But there are now generations growing up on video and computers, and they relate differently to the world, they read things differently. First of all they don't read really, they no longer have the patience. It's very visual and fast-paced, the way they try to take in the world.

Gass: Yes, and they will do well up to a point in the new community, but they can't think, so they won't rule. They are doomed. What is I think very likely to happen is that those who are good at the abstract manipulation of symbolic systems—and that's both visual and verbal, auditory, etc.—will be in the driver seat. This is a technological era where such abstract reasoning power is more important than ever. And it isn't just the ability to manipulate things—that will give you a nice medium-placed job, but it won't be where decisions are made. It will make some people who market that kind of stuff rich, but the ideas and the development of thinking about them and planning is going to be in the hands of the intellectual, the educated in this general sense, more than ever before. It's a dangerous result. There's going to be a bigger gap, between the average, ordinary people and gifted ones.

Q: All on the basis of intelligence, and nothing else.

Gass: Yes. I'm afraid so. It's a worrisome thing. And again, this is just a guess, but I'm certain that a lot of people are worried about that. One never knows for sure, but it looks like it. And if you're just merely a competitive person in the world and you feather your own nest, the fact that the youth are not reading is to your benefit. They're the more easily manipulated. If you're concerned only about that, then you're much better off. Don't be in any hurry to educate the masses, that's always been the principle. And it's going to be harder to really educate them now, because they're going to think—and people are going to try to persuade them—that all this other froth is unnecessary. But images don't explain things, they are just something more that needs to be explained. So, you're going to need the people who can do that.

Q: Is your way of reading influenced by the fact that in your formative years New Criticism and the idea of close reading was everywhere?

Gass: It certainly influenced me, it showed me how it should be done. But I also received a philosophical training which was analytic. I was trained in a positivist tradition, with great emphasis on logic, the philosophy of science, linguistic analysis, and the idea of very close reading. The two together certainly determined my attitudes. It is not entirely ideologically free, but reading, and the teaching of reading in this fashion, is in a certain sense to learn a technique, a methodology, rather than to be taught a metaphysics or a politics. That's why even now in universities, when we're trying to teach poetry, close reading is the only way to do it. If you start teaching ideas or ideology, you're not teaching the poem, and nobody learns about it. Also, intellectual fashions change. So you have existentialist readings, phenomenological readings, etc. But reading is still the same old thing: paying attention.

Q: You mentioned earlier that the best criticism comes from people who are also writers. Paul de Man says somewhere that real irony comes from people who are critics, philosophers as well as writers. Is there a special connection here, are your works also ironic?

Gass: Well, they're often ironic. But not nearly as ironic as others can become. I tend to champion certain kinds of things with a kind of old-fashioned enthusiasm, too. I'm ironic about the world, but I don't have the same kind of ambiguity about works of art. I know they're good, I'm not worried about that. I have a feeling I generally understand what a work is doing, and so they don't belong to some category of irony. But of course about human behavior—sure, I'm ironic. About science, I have—I think—a reasonable skepticism, but a great deal of conviction also that it grows in the right direction. I'm a person, I suppose, trained to value very highly the tradition of science and mathematics, as well as art, and to regard them as very closely connected. But I'm not a humanist. The areas of history and sociology and popular psychology are a morass of great problems. I tend to be more committed to those studies whose progress is clearly measurable.

Q: You value art more than reality.

Gass: Well, reality, is everywhere, but some things in reality are to human beings more important than other things. A particular kind of behavior or observation or data can be immensely more important than other kinds of observations and supporting some theory. It seems correct to say that this kind of data is more important than others. The world is full of trivial material, and what often artists tend to do, especially novelists and poets in modern times, is try to elevate the ordinary to a higher status. But it's generally not done in ordinary life, where things are treated with real contempt and indifference by and large. It's the artist and the scientist who pay attention in a different way to the world, and who are trying to learn from the world in a way that people interested in politics, power of various sorts, or making money, are not. Of course there are scientists who are just as commercial as anybody else. But a real scientist is somebody who is really paying attention to the world, and that requires a responsible treatment and a very responsible defence of what they come up with. That's my main objection to deconstruction, it is intellectually bankrupt. But the same thing is true of the artist and the mathematician, in a different mode: both have great loyalties to things that have nothing to do with their own immediate interests and egos. And while that detachment can happen among historians, it is rare, it is harder to maintain, and it is sometimes attacked as just being a bad business. I'm very impressed with the work of very fine mathematicians for example, and it can be very close to what artists do.

Q: There are several examples of transgressions like Lewis Carroll or some of the Tel Quel group.

Gass: Sure.

Q: By saying this you also seem to denounce self-referentiality, something you've been accused of.

Gass: Self-referentiality is very important. It's just that you don't determine the quality of the man and the system by its self-referentiality. It may be very useful, and many scientific theories, while they're certainly grounded in experience in various ways, have their own momentum. They have to keep in touch with it. It isn't that the literary work doesn't refer to the world, it sure does, so Henry James is writing about society, he indeed is. What about society is he writing? He's writing about the language system, the codes, the meaning, the signification, that you have to organize, too. So that's another language you have to deal with.

Q: You echo *The Tunnel:* "As I look at the pages of my manuscript, or stare at the books which wall my study, I realize I must again attempt to put this prison of my life in language." Is that what your work has been about?

Gass: Certainly my work has been about it, and it's been ambiguous about it. All my novels in particular have been about word-drunk people, who are basically dangerous. There is a tension between living a life and writing a life. It's important of course to write the life, but it's important to have a life to write. I've been interested in that kind of tension. I ran into it when I was young and reading people like Mann for whom it is a fundamental thing. There's nothing new about it, and nothing new about the dangers of having a skill to use literary techniques to create beliefs and start to act within a work of art as if it were reality. One of the things James does in his late novels is to point out the danger of treating people in terms of aesthetic categories. That becomes a part of the moral subject matter of a book like the *Golden Bowl, Wings of the Dove,* even as early as *The Spoils of Poynton* and a *Portrait of a Lady.* When he's doing this, he's adopting a certain kind of moral position, and one can disagree or agree with it, but he also takes the time to write a great book about it. And that's something that's always concerned me. I'm fascinated with rhetoric, rhetoric is a great thing. Eloquence is a wonderful thing. But eloquence doesn't prove anything, and people are swayed by those kinds of things to do things they shouldn't do.

Q: Is it like an underlying fascism, hidden in the nature of literature and fiction?

Gass: Yes, sure. It indeed has appealed to many that way. Most of the early

modernists were right-wing bigots of one sort or another, whether it's a Lawrence kind of fascist thing, or the socially neat little T. S. Eliot's or the worst,
Pound's. It's actually interesting that a lot of the painters were the same. Take
Degas, a really horrid little man, but what a painter! The problem was again,
this kind of aestheticising, and adapting, as Eliot did, religious points of view
for the sake of the poetry. The people who were free from that, people of a
different, left-wing ideology like Brecht, had a fascist element running all the
way through his high-mindedness. But their views were based on public performance. The architects tended to be left, the playwrights tended to be more
left-wing, and the poets and the painters the other way around. Now political
positions have completely changed in this country. Most writers are at least
liberals in some general, vague sense. One of my complaints against deconstruction is that it not only played with language, it started to make claims
on the basis of the play. There is a danger of fascism or some kind of totalitar-
ianism when people forget that their constructions are fictional.

Q: In *The Tunnel,* you write about the Holocaust using a special novelistic
form. *The Tunnel* is a novel of the historian Kohler who is writing it instead
of an academic study on guilt and innocence in Hitler's Germany from an
inexcusably forgiving perspective. Why did you turn to history, and why this
particular period?

Gass: I wanted to tackle a bunch of aesthetic issues I thought were crucial.
At the same time, again, it's the problem of language which history develops
more poignantly really than any other area because by and large history is
about what isn't there anymore. And so what is there? Sure, there remain
various kinds of things, but mostly texts. History is an attempt to create a
nontextual world from texts and by means of its own texts. There are dangers
and problems in doing that, especially when you have available to assist you
poetic and fictional devices, rhetorical structures as well. The theme that puts
the greatest stress on these temptations would be an event or a series of events
like the Holocaust. The Holocaust is interesting because it puts the greatest
amount of stress on philosophy, on political systems, on theology, on the
whole sense of the value of the nature of the human race as well as of course
on history itself. And so I get fascinated not so much with the Holocaust as
such, but with attempts to deal with it. For instance, there is a particular
problem for the Jews. How are they going to deal with a deity under whose
rule this happens? How are they going to include or encompass the Holocaust
as a historical event? And for many it's not an historical event, it falls outside

history. Because if it's an historical event, then the Holocaust that the Jews are concerned about is simply an extreme case of many such persecutions, both of Jews and non-Jews. It was just a bigger one than we've ever had; a catastrophic, huge, volcanic eruption. That then makes it just very big, but not unique. It's very important for a lot of people that the Holocaust be a unique occasion. Very special, set aside and particular for them, so to speak. And the odd thing is that it becomes the sacred event in this very curious way. Sacred too in the sense that it is especially significant only for some people, only for Jews, or only for Jews who have experienced its horrors are allowed even to talk about it. These are odd things. So, if the Holocaust is placed outside of history in order to preserve its uniqueness, it has nothing to say about history. If it's inside history, it's only another historical event. And that gives a rise to the possibility of weakening it, of making it "Gee, very big," but not extraordinary.

Q: Is this the first mistake Kohler makes? That he actually tries to take on this subject?

Gass: It's certainly the first mistake I made. The problem of understanding the Holocaust, or trying to, include the temptation to try to explain it away. But to set it outside of history is to explain it away. To normalize it in any sense is to explain it away. And we have these interesting books now coming out about how the German people often agreeably went along, and that kind of problem is a wonderful problem for a text, it enables me to come to grips with those issues. And because I give the problem to Kohler, I don't have to settle anything. I can talk about them, and maneuver and see how these things are used and developed ideas without taking a stand—saying this is the way it is, or was. But those who, like the teacher of Kohler in this book, say that history is basically textual and the best text wins, make a fascist move. It's their intention to allow history to move on without any connection to the old sense of what history was. The truth then disappears, and it only too often does. I'm old-fashioned in that sense, I think it's a calamity when it does. And I regularly run the risk of being said to have the same views that my narrator does.

Q: Though what I feel most fascinating about this book is how easy it is to get lost in enjoying its language; every part seems to be written with great fervor. Is that also a warning about how easy it is to cover up the real subject by the words and by indulgence in the text itself?

Gass: Yes, the technique is in part the seduction. Seducing the reader into starting to have sympathies about things which are not all that nice by the right kind of language. And that, of course, is a part of the theme. I am also taking a further step toward this identification by deliberately adopting certain modes of connecting myself with the text, with Kohler, that is. Similar Germanic name, things of this sort. The purpose of this is basically to suggest (which I do tend to think), that Kohler isn't just some peculiar monster, but is everyman. So the author, while he wants to detach himself from the narrator, cannot detach himself from the narrator completely, no more than anybody else can be detached from this narrator. Well, I'm going to get bashed for that.

Q: This is still a very risky subject to write about. So much has been said and written about the Holocaust, last year even the Hollywood blockbuster version, *Schindler's List,* came out. Apparently it is true that the more that is said about it, the further away it drifts.

Gass: Sure. Well, I have a particularly outrageous little section in which we end up admiring the Holocaust because it killed so many. You know, the "Oh, it killed six million!" I have this passage which says well, how many do we have to kill before we really get a Holocaust and not just a pogrom. This is a common thing. On holidays in this country, we break records for the number of people killed on the highways. Sure, people will go "Ccc, too bad, but gee we killed more people isn't that amazing?" We're obsessed with statistics. So, when somebody blows up the next building in this country, it will be "More people killed even than in Oklahoma!" It's just horrible, but it happens like this all the time, and the whole horror of the event will disappear into the talk. Which leads some people to say that we shouldn't talk about it, we mustn't talk about it. In some religions you're not allowed to utter the name of the deity. But it won't work. We need to keep it absolutely clear and present and have to get over it, but without altering or denying it.

Q: So is this a 700-page objection to the idea that the only adequate answer to the Holocaust is silence?
Gass: Oh sure, but of course the Holocaust has produced immense amounts of texts. Huge amounts, and will continue.

Q: Why are you sending this narrator underground?
Gass: Well, there's a long history of that, for many reasons and on many levels. We don't know he's underground, he is a liar. He might be making this up. Actually, there are all kinds of different tunnels, and I wanted all of

them. Some tunnels are tunnels that try to circumvent obstacles, some to escape, to mine, some to do other things. This is an activity which I wanted to put on a literal as well as a symbolic level. But I also wanted him to dig the tunnel just because it was fun.

Q: The tunnel is not an overused metaphor in literature. There are few works that employ it. How did you come up with the idea?

Gass: It was a while before I decided on the tunnel as the major image. And it's true, there have only been few books that have adopted that kind of imagery, but I didn't learn about almost any of them until later. Sábato has a novel called *The Tunnel,* and Dorothy Richardson, a woman who wrote a lot of long novels in the same period as Virginia Woolf, wrote *The Tunnel.* And of course Kellerman's novel, which was crucial for me, because Kellermann's novel was the novel that was made into a movie which was Hitler's favorite.

Q: *Der Tunnel,* yes.

Gass: There were popular uses of the tunnel in movies more than anywhere else. So called imaginative movies about the Transatlantic tunnel as well as movies just about digging tunnels under rivers. Tunnelling is important in American history. Then there is also a whole long tradition of the underground man.

Q: As this very patient narrator is digging his way through the tunnel, what we get is debris from his mind, bits and pieces of memory, and there's always the banality of these memories, the smallness like that of the sticker on an olive-oil bottle. Does this have something to do with the idea that evil ultimately reveals itself as something that is very banal?

Gass: That's part of the problem. The Hannah Arendt thesis is one of the things that are part of the novel's functioning elements. Also, once I had the imagery of the tunnel, it was not just to be something that happens in the book, or to be a metaphor of going through his past, digging through it. It gave me the three basic structures for the book. The book has to be a pile of dirt that he digs out. It has to be the hole, and I want to pun on that word, as it is both the unity and the emptiness. And finally, to build the tunnel you not only have to take the dirt away, and have an empty hole, but you have to prop it up, so it has to have a structure that holds the thing in place, to keep it from falling in. The structure of the book itself then became a tunnel. And the reader is going through the tunnel that has been dug with a corresponding adventure so to speak, since at one point the tunnel caves in, and so does the text. Sometimes it's easy to dig, sometimes it's harder. That kind of structure is developed out of the metaphor.

Q: You use a lot of typographical experimentation and pictures, like bits and pieces of the debris of the real; did you do that for the playfulness?

Gass: Well, I wanted the playfulness, or rather the privateness of it. There are textual parallels for the drawings. Some of the drawings are carry-overs and realizations of his fantasy about the party of the disappointed people. He then starts to design uniforms and stuff. The fact is that he doodles, the fact is that one whole aspect of his nature—the Culp character—is a constant reducer of everything to drivel.

Q: Did you actually make up those limericks?

Gass: Sure. It was quite a challenge to do all those limericks, "I once went to bed with a nun," right? And all of those, the puns, the drawings, some of which have to be in a certain way pointless, bothers the reviewers a lot. They say "What is this all about?" The point was first of all that the diagrams and the illustrations couldn't be professional, since this guy's doodling. And he's doodling and playing because the language does the same thing, and it's like drawing, playing tic-tac-to on a corpse. So it increases the indifference, the removal, the privateness, the withdrawn thing. The fact is that he's not writing a book, he's not trying to. The actual text is all the worse, because I wanted this to be clear that he's not writing something for publication, he's just in his own world. He made that hole in the ground. He's doing anything he pleases. Why not? Incorporating these is also some kind of an assault on the traditional structures of novels—this is very much an anti-novel, an anti-narrative novel. But behind all that, the imagery is very serious from my point of view. I'm not only interested in the play, I'm also interested in the handsome page. These squiggles are designed to do something to the page. Also, they're designed to increase the page-made notion of the book, so that it's not simply a run-on of passive reading. In a dense, long book like this they are also needed to breaking up the dense and defeating look of the text.

Q: It's a relief.

Gass: It's an important relief for the reader's eye. I've tried it before.

Q: Yes, when I bought *Willie Masters' Lonesome Wife,* the woman at the register must have thought it was something pornographic, and she called out to her colleagues. "Have a look at this!" I was tempted to tell her it's actually not about sex but about reading. Though it's been often said about you that you take a strongly eroticised look at texts, interpreting the relations between reader and text and writer and text in terms of love or six.

Gass: Yes, but it's certainly far from the conventional sense of the word. I'm certainly interested in that relationship, and I wrote *On Being Blue* about it. Erotic sensations are only an example for all of the feelings. All of them can be placed in a text, arousing readers, making them hungry. It might be something that you'd want to do in your restaurant review, and which many novels are aiming at. When most critics talk about a steamy sex scene in a book, they mean it's arousing. That is not what I have I mind at all. I don't disapprove, but it's not aesthetically proper. What I am trying to do is to get the sensuality into the language. And that sensuality does then transfer in an odd way. The writer has to have a sensual response to the concepts, and the language, and the sounds, and the look, everything that he's working with. The reader then responds, but not as if to the "real" thing. If I'm reading one of the great descriptive passages in D. H. Lawrence—and I think he is one of the greatest of our writers in this respect. I find that the language is so sensual, the perceptions are so marvelous, everything is so perfectly arranged, that it's just absolutely ravishing. And not arousing in the least in that sense. Lawrence is seeing the scene, and he's describing it, constructing this text in which the sensuality of the world is given to the language, and then you observe it as a reader. This skill concerns all the sensations, all the feelings: language has to contain the emotions. It's not enough just to arouse them. In a perverse way that's why I use a lot of limericks, because the limerick is a flatterer, the limerick destroys emotion, perhaps it produces giggles, but it is a downer. It's an interesting form for that reason. I wrote a few horrible limericks on Auschwitz. What a transgression! It made a lot of readers furious. From my point of view it is an essential transgression, and has to be performed. So there are passages in the book where I'm attempting to render the Culp version of things: other passages in which I'm attempting a more lyrical response to the same material. That's equally offensive to some people because Holocaust is too horrible to have a lyrical rendering in any part or fashion.

Q: How long have you been working on this book?

Gass: Twenty-six years. Not continuously, of course. The composition of the book was interrupted many times. I had rather long periods when I did nothing with it—as much as a year or two. I found it very hard to compose, and for a long time I was trying to figure out what I was really trying to do,

before I got at last the structure clear. Now the book is over-structured. It had
to look chaotic and wild while being as tightly bound as a body in a corset.
The oddest part about the composition of the book is that half of the material,
not the last half, but half of the bulk of the text, was written in one year. 600
pages. I had a year off, and after 25 years of preparation, I did nothing but
write, and I wrote 600 pages. It's scattered around through the book, a great
bulk of it is toward the end, where the style for the most part gets smoother,
more narrative, and more propulsive.

Q: Are you the first critic of your work?

Gass: You have to be. I mean, it's tricky, because your whole critical
maneuvering may be to hide what you've really done. A book takes a long
time, and it's complicated. You have to have a grip on it. Not only do you
have to have an intellectual framework to enable you to go back to it and
enter the same structure, but you have to have a narrator or some dominant
tone that is strong enough to recapture. If it isn't very strong, then you will
lose the book. You will have changed, still, you have to go back and enter
that world which you started 20 years before. And the only way that re-entry
can be accomplished is if you have a strong enough, intellectually describ-
able, structure, and a clearly defined and powerful consciousness. It's not
pleasant; that character was not a place one enjoyed being. Sometimes I did
enjoy it, but most of the time I did not.

Q: You say the book is over-structured but still chaotic.

Gass: The world is chaotic but often looks ordered. The book had to look
chaotic, but be designed. I want to be able to fit everything into the novel's
system. I wrote the early section and later on broke it up into pieces. They
were more unitarian initially. Later the units began to cohere, and larger and
larger sections were continuous. But I deliberately disheveled it and intro-
duced all kinds of other things like repetitions, contradictions. Those operate
only on one level, but each anomaly has to have a justification within the
larger structure, so the larger structure must mimic human memory, human
consciousness. It lies, it forgets and contradicts. It's fragmentary, it doesn't
explain everything, doesn't even know everything. These ordinary human
difficulties had to be present in the book, just from the realistic point of view,
let alone the other oddities I wanted to add. But then the question was, all
right, you have all those elements you want to put in the book, but how,
when, where, why? The book also has the idea that it's very likely that all
the characters this narrator talks about are elements of his own nature, iso-

lated elements of a particular side of him. He obviously has a Culp side. After all, where is Culp coming from? That notion requires the splitting of the self. Then I carefully kill off those characters at certain points, so that they disappear. Well, I had to ultimately organize the novel in terms of a model gained from Schoenberg: 12 sections, 12 tone system, that is how I began working out the way the various themes come in and out. It's layered that way too, and there are other things trying to hold it together. *The Tunnel* is supposed to be a mass made of orders.

Q: Do you ever read the criticism about your works?

Gass: I'm curious enough to see it. I don't read long articles, I just get bored, I can't help it. I try to be as conscious about what I am doing as possible, but when I'm reading the criticism, I'm either reading somebody explaining to me what I already know, or telling me something I think is wrong, and neither of these is of much interest. It is especially sad to read critics who try to treat a nontraditional, non-narrative novel as if it were telling the same old story. That means you haven't succeeded. But I do look at them, though I wouldn't say I really read them. It doesn't matter, nothing anybody says changes the book one way or another, makes it better or worse.

Q: Martha Kohler's wife says at one point that the reason he can't stop is that then he'd have nothing to do.

Gass: Well, that's certainly part of it. Then it's of course a kind of Beckett-situation: "I can't go on. I must go on. I have no reason to go on." But in fact the book comes to an end, I finished it, one way or another.

Q: Are you saying that the life of this narrator-writer, and perhaps the lives of all writers last as long as their teas?

Gass: Sure. You may deliberately wish to rescue the world by putting it in language, but you're certainly burying yourself in it. The book's become your tomb, you know. There you are, for better or worse. It's all you are, and all you will be, eventually. And I think that the book won't be what you were. It is something you made, but not what you were.

Q: Does it bother you that people will remember you on the basis of the books you wrote?

Gass: I hope they do. But once you're dead, it doesn't matter at all. It's only when you're thinking about it now. Now it's nice to think that somebody may read them, and still could continue to read them for a while. The grave, though, contains only your bones and none of your fears, hopes or worries.

Q: Are you currently working on something?

Gass: Well, I have a book coming out this fall, just another collection of essays. It's hard to get anything new done during school-year, but I'm working on a collection of short stories, and a book on Rilke, and a book on photography, and the next one to come out should be is on the relation of architectural structure to fictional structure. All these texts have grown over many years, except the collection of short stories, and they are almost done. The essay collection was nearly done when I published *The Tunnel*. I just needed to do a few things to rewrite the essays. The architecture book is almost completed, and the photography book is mostly done, too.

Q: Do you have preferences for some of your works?

Gass: Well, fiction is what I really want to write. However, it is harder, and people are less interested in it, they really prefer my essays. Fiction is far more important to me. But it's not been easy to do because I need long stretches of time and total emersion to work on fiction.

Q: 26 years, that is a bit extreme.

Gass: Yes, it is, but all my books, even the books of essays, from the first essay to the last, would almost always take at least ten years to write. Perhaps I'm slow.

Q: Perhaps you have the patience of the digger of the tunnel.

Gass: Well, it's partly patience, but you have to figure in the way you live. I get interested in new things all the time—distracted—and then, I leave something when it gets hard, to move on to something else. *The Tunnel* was a great avoidance book. I wrote other books in order to avoid writing it. I always have been bouncing about. But I didn't work on Rilke for 40 years, and now I'm almost done with the translations of the *Elegies* which will form a central part of the text. It will be a short book, thank heaven. I do require a long gestation, it takes me a forever to figure out what I want to do. And I've never been in any hurry: I didn't publish my first book until after I was 40.

Q: That I guess is a pretty non-American way of looking at things.

Gass: Yes, but almost all of my models are European. I've had American writers who were enormously influential for me, Gertrude Stein is a good case, but reading Flaubert's letters was one of the crucial things. It told me what kind of a writer to be, though he also belonged to a previous generation. The writers I admire from my own generation were all after the great book. You know, Gaddis, Barth, etc., they were all working for the supreme achievement. Writing is not an amusement for them, it was a very serious business. And the writers that I admire, whether they write long, big books or not, have that ambition of looking at their career as a life devoted to certain projects. Sure you'd like to be successful, but that's not the issue. Such attitudes have mostly disappeared. Actually *The Tunnel* was attacked, among other reasons, for the fact that it was seen as a '60s book rewritten in the '90s. Because the '60s saw the last of the big books. The Latin-American big books and the Americans, *The Sot-Weed Factor,* and all those enormous things. The ambition to write big books or the willingness to take the time, that was rampant in the '60s.

Q: By saying "big," do you mean just the format, the number of pages?

Gass: Just the importance, the ambition of the project. I mean, anybody can run on and on—I've been accused of that, too. And of course this kind of ambition . . . you are not going to win to achieve your aim. But it used to be a part of a serious writer. So everybody who was a writer was trying to do something important—and not just to gain renown or get into the *New Yorker.* Even to get an identity as a writer was a terribly important business. And I still feel that way. It goes further back than the sixties, it's nineteenth century romanticism about the artist; it is a very romantic but not a rosy view.

Something in the World Worth Having: An Interview with William H. Gass

Ronald Spatz / 1997

From *AQR: Alaska Quarterly Review,* 15.3&4 (1997), 9–14. Reprinted by permission.

AQR: How do you assess the vitality of the novella form as it relates to the novel and the short story?

Gass: Well, that's a difficult question, because the novella has always been regarded as a kind of sport, not a main thing, neither short nor long and so without definition. But I think in a way it's the ideal length for the kind of prose which wishes to achieve real, continued tension, the kind of tension that you expect say from poetry or short story, but has ambitions for a longer range. Novellas, I think, are in general far more powerful and have more potentiality for experiment than the short story. I'm thinking of some of the best of Faulkner and James. The novella gives you room to really reach for the moon but you're not going to take years to get there.

AQR: In an essay in the *New York Times Book Review* you made the point that "fiction is an exploration, and exploration is the work of a realist, however fanciful that reality might seem to those encountering it for the first time."

Gass: There are two senses of that word *realist* here. First of all, when you're talking about something being exploratory there has to be something *real* that you're exploring. Otherwise, the exploration is meaningless. There are two kinds of realism involved. The first is the reality of the medium and the object you're making, which you are in a sense exploring in order to create. That is particularly true with what's called experimental fiction, because what you're doing is exploring the nature and character of the art itself and finding out things that are real and possible. There's no better proof that something can be done in literature than by doing it, and no better proof that a rule that says you can't do it is a bad rule than by breaking it and succeeding. The second notion of reality involves the view that fiction creates a reality, and that reality has in many ways more power than what we com-

138

monly call real life and day-to-day existence. Artistic reality is repeatable. It constantly grows richer. It stays around. It doesn't disappear. That's why great texts have more reality than the things they're usually about. The situations the texts are about pass away; the texts remain and reoccur.

AQR: Within the context of experiment versus the tried and true, how do you view the usefulness of the traditional forms of fiction—those with a beginning, middle, and an end?

Gass: It's gotten so that trying to write something with a beginning, middle and an end would be experimental again. The people who are trying to do the traditional thing are very often writers without great ambition or even skills, though they may appeal to popular taste. But I think it's still possible to exploit very traditional strategies and to discover new things in those techniques; however, it takes a serious writer of great skill to do it now. It's too easy to fall into the cliches of the tradition when you go back to it. That's always a risk. It would be quite a challenge to just sit down and try to write a nice Victorian story. But, of course, there's no point in writing one that just passes back into the past as if it had been written there. It has to be revivified, put to new uses. So, I would regard a first class writer returning to traditional narrative as taking on an experimental task.

AQR: Do you agree with what Leslie Fiedler once termed "the moral dimension of form"?

Gass: There is a moral dimension to form. There's no doubt about that. I'm not sure if I have the same sense of it that Fiedler does. But the difference, I think, has been put very well by Theodor Adorno. He preferred the twelve tone breakthrough to the Stravinsky eclecticism. A truly revolutionary writer should demolish old forms and constitute new ones. It doesn't do any good to have a revolution in which you just take one set of bureaucrats out of office and put in another set, and the same is true with literature. You aren't a revolutionary writer if you suddenly write a novel about masturbation or some other shocking subject, because it's the same old novel in a different shirt. Similarly ninety percent of the so-called left wing novels are written in right wing, bourgeois form. The form undercuts the propaganda. The form is the determinate thing, and the other is just the dressing. So if you want to be a moral innovator, you'll have to innovate formally. One of the earlier mistakes the Marxists made was to concentrate on content. Later Marxists realized that the message doesn't realize the revolution. However, the fact that you use a revolutionary form doesn't mean the work is going to be automatically any good. And if you create great things in traditional modes as Stravinsky certainly did, more power to you.

AQR: As a stylist, your fiction has been praised for rising to an almost spiritual level—that your sentences have "souls."

Gass: I wrote an essay once called "The Soul Inside the Sentence" and then in the new book *Finding a Form* there are a couple of pieces that talk about books as containers of consciousness. Good writing has to have the qualities we associate with a rich awareness. It has to have something parallel to desire, parallel to perception, parallel to emotion, parallel to thought, parallel to imagination. A sentence has got to see well; it has to feel powerfully; it has to have an urgent character. I don't mean it must always be rushing, but it must have a deep and satisfying movement. And it has to be excellent in the combination of concepts. Let's say your imaginative side is in the metaphorical the allegorical element of the sentence. Then there's the conceptual structure, next the musical element, and so on. All of these elements combine to create a linguistic consciousness. So when I listen to Bach, for example, my mind moves as those notes move, and when reading a great poet, my mind moves as those words do. But those words create a consciousness both of the world and of feeling, of desire and of imagination at the same time.

AQR: One of the compelling aspects of your work is your use of setting— the vividness, albeit cold and unrelentingly bleak, of America's heartland.

Gass: First of all, the setting doesn't always happen in ordinary life to harmonize with one's mood or action. But any fictional environment has to be totally functional and symbolic. It has to in a sense develop, and be appropriate to, what takes place within it. Or, you may want to play a game and create a somber setting for something that is fundamentally gay and light hearted. The landscape that I work with—the weather and the geography— are designed to be projections of the interior state of the individual or the meaning of the scene. The actual Midwest landscape is by turns cold and beautiful, and like fall here now it's not snowing as in Anchorage—the leaves are just drifting down here, and it's 72 degrees and gorgeous. But, of course, you know it may rain in the heart if it rains in the town. That's the idea. So if my, scenery is bleak, it's because the meaning or the characters' souls are. It doesn't mean the Midwest is. The Midwest is too complex for climate.

AQR: Concerning matters of the heart?

Gass: They're usually matters having to do with love, friendship, fidelity to things, the courage of convictions. They are the most serious issues involving basically the nature of human relations. And I tend to work with people or characters who have aspirations, have potentiality, which for one reason or another has not been realized, and they are painfully aware of that. This then produces a conflict, a dismay that one's qualities have not been fulfilled, that one's fallen far short of what might have been. And this is particularly true concerning the ability to feel, to see, to respond. To have had a life and not enjoyed it is a terrible thing. My fictions explore such disappointments largely from within, rather than from without, as in, "I had a life, but didn't enjoy it because capitalism was oppressive." Such oppression certainly happens, but I'm much more interested in how we are the enemies of ourselves. People are constantly betrayed by other people too, but one rises above these things if one is strong enough, and my characters usually aren't.

AQR: How can you bear that kind of truth? Twenty-six years of writing *The Tunnel* and there's no way out.

Gass: I'm just being as honest as I can. There isn't any way out, except the grave. That seems to me a realistic point of view. I don't think love is redemptive unless it's the love of, as Spinoza says, things that won't betray you. There aren't very many things in this world that loyal. I do think that a lot of science and mathematics can be reasonably relied on, and I think a lot of art commands that respect. When you're reading a really great writer, you may be in the hands of someone who, as a person, is mean and spiteful, but because the art is exemplary, so are those transformed hands. Art is one of the few good things human beings do in the world even if what is being written is also an indictment of mankind. That's what I answered when somebody at a French magazine once asked me, "Why do you write?" "I write to indict mankind." Maybe it was a smartass remark, but it expresses my point of view. If the indictment is phrased properly, then, although it won't reform mankind or redeem me, at least I will have left something in the world that's worth having, something that wouldn't have been there otherwise, something perhaps sad, but savvy. And that's about all one can do.

AQR: So the light at the end of *The Tunnel* are rays of truth?

Gass: Well, if it is the truth. One of the themes of my work is that people certainly do not want to know the truth, and they construct all sorts of idiocies to avoid facing it. But you can face the truth the way Russell does in *A Freeman's Worship:* "Thought looks into the pit of hell, and is not afraid." Of course, that's a romance of Reason. But there's a kind of exultation that comes from having a mind, as Dr. Johnson would say, free of cant, free of superstition, free of illusion.

Still Digging: A William Gass Interview

Richard Abowitz / 1998

From *Gadfly,* Dec. 1998. Reprinted by permission.

William Gass may well be our greatest living writer. Gass first achieved fame thirty years ago with the publication of the short story collection *In the Heart of the Heart of the Country* (Harper & Row, 1968). These stories, heavily influenced by the prose of Gertrude Stein, are still among the most anthologized and admired in contemporary fiction. The same year, the journal *Tri-Quarterly* published *Willie Masters' Lonesome Wife* in which Gass used games, photography, footnotes and a coffee stain to subvert—in, to be candid, a rather dated 60s way—the fictional process by bringing the reader into a metafictional maze of self-referentiality. However, Gass's most outrageous accomplishment is a project that consumed him for close to three decades: his second novel *The Tunnel* (Knopf, 1995).

A few words on *The Tunnel's* plot are in order. William Frederick Kohler, the narrator, is a middle-aged professor of history who has recently finished writing his masterpiece: *Guilt and Innocence in Hitler's Germany.* Filled with bitterness, envy, rage and misanthropy, Kohler sits down to write the preface and spews out *The Tunnel's* 650 pages. The book's title arises when Kohler for no particular reason and to no particular purpose decides to dig a tunnel in the basement of his suburban Midwestern house.

The Tunnel may well be the greatest prose performance since Nabokov's *Pale Fire,* but only the most stalwart reader will be able to last the full trip through Kohler's anti-Semitic, sexually depraved and bathroom-humor obsessed world. When *The Tunnel* was published, almost every major critic felt the need to weight in on it. Many abandoned their professional tone and responded in ways that were shockingly personal.

"This is the most vexing reviewing assignment I've ever undertaken," Sven Birkerts confessed in the *Atlantic Monthly.* In the *National Review* James Bowman called *The Tunnel* "a load of crap." But a *Los Angeles Times* critic called it "the most beautiful, most complex, most disturbing novel to be published in my lifetime."

142

Born in Fargo, North Dakota, in 1924 and raised in Ohio, Gass has spent most of his life in the Midwest, a region he famously loathes and that forms the backdrop for much of his fiction. Since 1969 he has taught philosophy at Washington University in St. Louis, where he is currently director of the International Writers Center. *Gadfly* spoke to William Gass shortly before the release of *Cartesian Sonata: and Other Novellas,* his first fiction since *The Tunnel.*

Richard Abowitz: Was most of *Cartesian Sonata: and Other Novellas* written before *The Tunnel* was completed?

William Gass: Oh, no, just one was written a long time ago in rough draft. That was the first piece—called in the book "Cartesian Sonata." The rest, the last three, which are designed to match the first one, were written in the last year. I have a long span of gestation, I guess. The last story, "The Master of Secret Revenges," for example, was an idea maybe 35–40 years ago and then just sat there not doing a thing until recently. The other two, "Bed and Breakfast" and "Emma Enters a Sentence of Elizabeth Bishop's," were more recent and don't appear to have had any lengthy sort of time in my unconscious, but you never know about those things.

RA: Elizabeth Bishop isn't the sort of writer you usually focus on. Did you know her?

WG: No, I didn't know her personally and I was slow to come to her work. Out of that group of people—Lowell, Jarrell, Roethke, Berryman and so on—I was reading them more than her at first. So it was a little slow, but now I think she is the most important of all.

RA: What is it about Bishop's work that appeals to you?

WG: Absolute precision, and an extraordinary care with everything. A marvelous perception. Here is a case sort of like Henry James where no idea violates it, but there are plenty of ideas lying behind the surface of the work.

RA: Has the computer changed how you write? When you started *The Tunnel,* there were no word processing computers right?

WG: Right. No, I worked from a very early age on a typewriter which I was given—a little portable—so I was in one sense prepared for the computer because I never wrote by hand. It proved to be a godsend actually because I was able to write much more rapidly on it and was able to complete *The Tunnel* in a year, writing about half of it in that last year on the computer.

RA: You wrote that much of it in the last year?

WG: Yes. I had written about 600 pages of *The Tunnel* in manuscript and I wrote about 600 pages more to finish up what I had planned: 12 sections about 100 pages each. These measurements, of course, are all manuscript measurements.

RA: One of the things I noticed in reading *The Tunnel* is that you frequently make use of—I don't mean in the limericks—poetic meter in your prose.

WG: Oh, yes, I tend to employ a lot of devices associated with poetry. Not only metrical, but also rhyme, alliteration, all kinds of sound patterning. I also borrow a great deal from rhetoric and rhetorical structures.

RA: In Watson Holloway's book on you, he says that you advocate experimental writing more in your criticism than you practice it in your fiction. Do you think that is accurate?

WG: No. I assume that's one of the troubles people have with it: it is too experimental. I do a lot more experimenting in the fiction than in the essays. But it isn't something that I think is a requirement for a writer. It is just something that interests me.

RA: When you were preparing to publish *The Tunnel,* were you worried about being compared to Kohler, about people seeing the book as somehow autobiographical?

WG: Not worried so much. I knew it would happen. The book does set a number of traps for reviewers, and that identification certainly occurred. But the book in sly ways even encourages it; so that these people who don't really know how to read will fall into the trap. It was just an amusement on my part, and so when it happened, I had to suffer it. I had asked for it in a way.

RA: One of those reviewers who fell into the trap would then be Robert Alter, who accused *The Tunnel* of being an immoral book because it compares Nazi persecution to domestic trauma.

WG: Yes, well, that is one way he wants to interpret it, but, of course it is, and must be, to some sorts of reader an immoral book. I want it to be for them. I want it misread in a certain way by certain people. It's for me the proof of the pudding. Alter has a certain sacred cow—I mean, the Holocaust. I don't think anything is sacred and therefore I am prepared to extol or make fun of anything. People who have very settled opinions are going to dislike this book because Kohler is the worm inside all of that stuff.

RA: What is your view of Kohler?

WG: Well, I think he is every complex. I tried to make him a very sophisticated complex humanist in such a way as to exhibit one of the crucial problems of the whole Nazi period, and that is that there was no profession, no level of education, no quality and sensitivity, which can protect you from that virus. So I had to make him somebody who would even, from time to time, show sufficient sensitivity and regard so that the reader would begin to move along in his mind track. Then, of course, derailment occurs. He is also for me a model of a kind of mind that is very common in the United States: a slightly hidden Fascist mentality.

RA: How did you feel about the public reaction to *The Tunnel?* Were you surprised? What did you expect when it came out, and were you expecting the public to be shocked?

WG: No, I expected to be ignored. I mean, I expected a few critics to be shocked and upset, and indeed a few were. There were some who were quite enthusiastic, but by and large it was the usual: just shrugs and nobody paid much attention. There were a few outraged voices, but that didn't surprise me. I don't expect much response from the kind of thing I do. If I was looking for plaudits, then I really have done the wrong thing.

RA: Do you think the serious novel still has a role to play in our culture?

WG: I don't know about "role"—as if it acted, it went about doing things. It has a serious role to play in the very nature of existence, I think. Any serious art does. But as an actor on the stage of human affairs in the ordinary sense, I don't think so. I'm not one who thinks that one's life should be directed by art. It's simply one of the things that makes life bearable, but it doesn't give it purpose or direction. One's consciousness is filled with beauty perhaps (in the old sense), but hardly with truth and goodness. I would be terrified if I thought that, as Yeats worried, books or poems sent people out to do anything or led to people having certain kinds of convictions. That would also indicate that they have very weak minds.

RA: As a writer, you have chosen a different path, almost a hostile path to that little sub-group that is our literary culture. You don't teach in an MFA program, you don't even teach in an English department, and your essay on the Pulitzer certainly guarantees that you are completely outside of the log rolling in contemporary literature. I was wondering if this was just how your life developed, or whether at some point you decided you didn't want to be part of the mainstream.

WG: Well, I certainly decided very early I didn't want to be a part of any English department. I really don't get along with those people. I prefer to be in a place where one is teaching stuff meant to be taught. Philosophy is perfect that way. It is material meant to be chewed over and talked about and debated, and I enjoy that very much. Whereas, not certainly all, but many of the people in the English departments I find simply not caring about litera-ture, and just playing around with bad ideas. So I am grateful to be out of that region, and that was a decision I made very early. I've hardly ever studied literature seriously academically. I stayed away from it.

RA: Do you read many contemporary novels? Are there young writers that you like?

WG: I have tried to keep up somewhat because the Center is interested in finding young people who show promise. I have a model staff who points me in the right direction. I think it important to try to find out what's going on. I used to do that by agreeing to judge say the National Book Award or some-thing and then you'd get a dose of what was going on for at least a year. That was helpful even though it was painful as well: a lot of work. But, you know, you get distracted, you have too many other things to do, you don't read the way you used to for pleasure, you are always reading because you are review-ing. I no longer review anybody I'm likely ever to meet or be friends with or anything of the sort, and if I were ever to review a young person's book, I would be even more besieged by people wanting me to give them a lift. This is one of the disagreeable parts of this business. Everybody is after you for favors.

RA: Do you see your influence at all among younger writers?

WG: No, I don't. They are doing different things, and I think that is fine. I don't want anybody being influenced or following me. If I detected it I would drop the book in horror.

RA: What are your writing habits like now?

WG: I am an early riser, and I work mostly in the morning. I am usually through any serious writing by noon. When I am teaching, of course, that's a little altered, but I only teach one semester a year. I do my work at the Center in the afternoon and other kinds of work which is more mechanical.

RA: In a number of your books, your characters like to write naked. That's not true of you I assume?

WG: No. No. I have air conditioning. I don't have to take my clothes off.

RA: *Willie Masters' Lonesome Wife* was before contemporary graphic programs. I was wondering how you did the layout on that.

WG: This book was written for myself. I never expected anybody to publish it in any form. It was a very complicated text which could only be partially realized by any publisher, not only because some things were just simply impractical or impossible to do, but the rest, many of them, too expensive. Some ideas like setting the quotes that I interwove in the text in the type of the first edition of the book in which they appeared, that kind of thing was more a conceptual notion. It would have looked terrible and so there were other reasons for restraining. I worked with the designer on this who was, of course, trying to achieve what I wanted with good design and within budget.

RA: So there is no manuscript lying around with the coffee mark on it?

WG: Yes, there is. The original manuscript with the original notions and scribbles is at Washington University.

RA: What are you working on now?

WG: A book called *Reading Rilke* should come out next year. I'm trying to get rid of his ghost. It involves a translation of the poems, but as I am going through I talk about Rilke, language and the problems of translation. So it's also a little book about translation.

RA: Then are you working on a book about architecture?

WG: Architectural form and its relation to literary form. The structure of the sentence, the structure of the novel and the architecture of things. Architects deal with relations almost completely—how these relations are materially embodied. That is what interests me.

RA: What about fiction projects?

WG: I have another collection of novellas under way, and I'm about halfway done with another collection. I am not going to write any more novels. That takes me forever. I'm not going to do that.

RA: It seems like you have been incredibly productive since finishing *The Tunnel.* Did getting that out of the way just . . .

WG: I has been odd. In my 70s, I have been productive, but in a way I'm bringing to a close things that have been going on for a long time. I am trying to get them done and out of the way so that I can go on to some new things that I hope to fiddle with.

RA: Will that be in your 80s?

WG: I feel as young as I ever have, I guess. I am fortunate about that. My energy level seems not to have flagged. I'm still busy turning out stuff, but it may be that I will start slowing down when I don't have something that has been lying around for decades. New stuff might have to get old and I may not have time for that.

Interview with William Gass

Theodore G. Ammon / 2000

Unpublished interview conducted in St. Louis, Missouri, July 19, 2000.
Transcribed by Dora Robertson.

Q: How has your concept of metaphor changed since you wrote your dissertation?

Gass: It hasn't changed as much as expanded or gotten more elaborate. In my dissertation I didn't have a true interactive view of metaphor, and I didn't have the conception of metaphor as the intermeshing of a whole set of meanings, a whole range, or possible range of, anything represented by the token. It could be several concepts but in a whole history of them. I spent so much time on the historical conception, which is very thin and relatively mechanical, that I ended up with was a notion of the one term of the metaphor used as a lens through which to see the other term and then the more complex where they took turns being lens and object. So that suddenly one term and all that it may possibly refer to is used to interpret another meaning. That's what's behind basically the let's say renaissance notion of a conceit, where you say my love's body is a field. So if you use that kind of relationship, you can also use visual metaphors in that way. For instance, in *Endgame* when there are people living in the ash cans—that is a visual metaphor. It says something about the nature of life and it reinterprets the words 'living arrangement' or whatever you want to call it, in terms of all of the references of the ash can and that was my conception of what a metaphor was up to. But it's really producing an enormous number of little ones.

Q: And now . . . ?

Gass: Well, that's what I've come to now. It was much more mechanical. I didn't see it then as sufficiently interpretive of the whole thing, as rearranging the whole scheme, partly because a lot of people who use metaphors as soon as they make the connection, squeeze the thing together. They don't really mean the image even though they use the formal relationship.

Q: Several things come to mind, the first of which is Rorty's book *Philosophy and the Mirror of Nature* in which he trips back through the history of philosophy and teases out fundamental metaphors that have informed epistemology. Now it seems to me his argument cuts both ways; on the one hand we can disabuse ourselves of this metaphorical language and get at epistemology and on the other hand, given what Rorty has written later, it seems as if that's a hopeless enterprise and that we're never going to get out of metaphorical language. So is there really a serious distinction that can be drawn between the metaphorical and the non-metaphorical?

Gass: Well, serious, yes, but that would be for me formal. What you're suggesting is that the serious problem would have to be whether it is being correct or true or interpretable and a sort of single meaning or something of the sort, but the difference between let's say so called literal and figurative language has always been for me a fundamentally syntactical, or semantic one rather. Well, they're syntactical, pragmatic and semantic metaphors based on a violation each time of a principle. "After I kicked John in the teeth, I took off my hat." This is a violation of a pragmatic thing where taking off the hat is a sign of reverence or respect, so it's a pragmatic principle that's being broken. I could on the other hand assert something that is semantically impossible: "raining cats and dogs." And then there are the syntactical ones: "I was bitten by several round squares." I mean, any number of syntactical violations would produce one. "Any one lived in a pretty how town" Cummings writes; that's a syntactical metaphor. That's the principle of creating the figurativeness that is based on breaking a rule. So I've always held that the figurativeness involves a breach of one or the other, or all three sometimes, of these principles. And then the question is why does one go to a violation of any one of these standard norms in order to say something else? Why do you say "Richard is a lion," which is semantically impossible, when you could say "Richard is brave," which is literal and doesn't violate a principle? Now if you said "Richard is a horse's ass," you've already violated a principle and you've got a metaphor. But you could have said "Richard is the king of Belgium" and that would just simply be false. I mean it's a literal statement. There are all kinds of literal statements that don't even make a whole lot of sense sometimes but they're not violating a principle of some sort. Now then the question is: is there something about the structures both of society or of truth as it's understood or the syntactical rules or the grammatical rules that we can't get away from and we have to constantly reach for some new thing by violating them, but I don't know of a metaphor that would normally be recognized as a metaphor that doesn't violate one of those principles.

Q: But principles which are conventional and of—

Gass: Well, the pragmatic one, the so-called pragmatic one, is a conventional violation, a conventional rule, and it's often one of manners—

Q: There are certain things that one just doesn't say, in other words?

Gass: One doesn't . . . well, or backward or wrong. Often, for example, a pragmatic metaphor would be "He gave you the high hat." No, it really means you were snubbed. But then why would you go to an image which involves, let's say, dressing up and being high society and having a top hat, or something of the sort? And then moving to that kind of image in order to say he snubbed me? Then the question arises about the necessity to invoke such violations of language in order to do epistemology. Or is, as Borges has said, all metaphysics is based on six root metaphors? All philosophy or meta-physics can be reduced to things like "The world is a stage" or Borges in his view, "The universe is a library." Once upon a time, when was it, maybe in the thirties, Steven Pepper, wrote a book called *World Hypotheses,* in which he attempted to reduce all philosophical systems to I think maybe five root metaphors. And then there are a lot of people who say that the only way to get at or to try to render certain kinds of experience, is by wrenching lan-guage out of its normal mode. Mystics often say that, or they go further and say you can't say anything. So if someone wants to say that if we can't get away from the metaphor, then that means we can't escape, then in order to say something about this subject we have to formulate it in terms of a thing that violates what we expect at any rate, in terms of one or other of these three realms. It seems to me odd.

Q: We can't escape from metaphor . . . might be seen as something to lament but it's the flip side of not being able to escape the literal. And now Wittgenstein comes to mind. He seems to give us the world early in the *Tractatus:* The world is all that is the case. It is the totality of facts not things. I can grab hold of it but as one gets to the end we find out that the world is my world and the limits of language are the limits of my world. It turns out that you can climb up the ladder and get some sort of perspective perhaps but you are not going to be able to say what it is.

Gass: Yeah.

Q: We're stuck in language, in other words.

Gass: Yeah and we have a lot of things we should not bother talking about. Science for example is full of metaphor, mathematics is full of it, but when one makes these new things, is it ultimately that the thing becomes dead? It's really replacing a non-existent term, or really suggesting the need for a new term and so forth. All of these kinds of situations arise I think, and I think the imagery, or metaphorical language, is doing something quite different than those enterprises and you could start out by creating an image and then sorting through and discarding and reducing what you initially had in mind to something literal, but that is harder to do with syntactical violations, however; or even such things that we sometimes used to think were informative: "Business is business," something like that, but again a tautology which is nevertheless interpreted as saying much more. "Boys will be boys," and so on, you know.

Q: I think I'm agreeing with Quine on this, that they would presuppose some notion of synonymy of meaning, which even repetition, syntactical repetition, doesn't catch. "When they're gone they're gone" is not repetitious—

Gass: No not as it's interpreted. If "When they're gone they're gone" is just a straight tautology then nobody finds it in the least bit informative. It isn't, because it is tautology. But if it's really not a tautology then that is to say it's metaphorical. Now if it's metaphorical it's taking the rule of identity and violating it basically by using it. So that's what I mean, that even if you use a tautology in form you can still be breaking the syntactical rule, because you don't really mean it's equivalent.

And usually when you do that, and I'm not talking about puns like "The White House is really white" because that isn't really an equivalence, you're trading on the ambiguity. But usually your reply, let's say that "Business is business," is to insist that the concept "Business" we are in is one are going to stay in, that realm of values and structures is where we are discussing things and that's where we're going to stay. And you're wandering away. It's usually a reprimand in a certain sense. I mean I start to bring up some ethical issue and someone says "Business is business."

Q: And that's a reprimand—

Gass: Yeah, well if they're going to be a business man then you ought to think this way but if you want to go off and not do business, then all right, but business is business. Or somebody says that we have to cut down the amount of violence in football. Well, "Football is football," you know, that sort of thing. So as long as you're really going to cut down the violence is not to play football and so forth. To be ethical is not to do business and that sort of thing. It uses this simple formula to say quite a bit, actually, which couldn't be said as succinctly; but you can always unpack all that stuff. Now the question is when you're unpacking, my argument in the dissertation, I think, would still be my position, is that you have a real metaphor and you start unpacking it in terms of literal relationships, you are no longer really unpacking the metaphor. The metaphor when unpacked will just give you a lot of subordinate images. Now you can always reduce this but then you are just leaving the image . . . the image always means something else in addition.

Q: Ok. If I could segue from the discussion of metaphor to some of the nasty things that have been said about the way in which you handled the Holocaust—for example and for the record I'll read from this review: "The real obscenity of his novel [*The Tunnel*] is not its hideous language or its scatological imaginings but its trivialization of the enormity of genocide by absorbing it into the nickel-and-dime nastiness that people perpetrate in everyday life."[1] One of my first responses to that sentence was that person hasn't read Hannah Arendt and if he has he missed the point about the banality of evil. But a fundamental precept was missed in this statement.

Gass: A lot, actually, yeah.

Q: The difference between metaphor and what's metaphorical, what's literal and what's real—one has to hold on to the real. It demands a certain respect, a certain reverence, a certain ethical attitude and you have fundamentally violated, not simply syntactical or semantical rules, but you you've violated how we should think about the Holocaust.

Gass: Yeah, well that's one of the things. The first thing that is odd about this statement I think is the author of the book that he should be addressing is Kohler. (laughs) They never do that; I mean they never say this guy does such and such and such. No, it's always *me* you know, and so that's the first interesting thing. The second: part of the time what I want Kohler to be doing is exactly this diminishment. And then the character Culp is an even greater diminishment, because he is doing the limerical history of the world. But the other thing that's curious about the Holocaust is that it is an enormity which has become sacred, and only Jews, only Jews of a certain sort, are allowed really to talk about it: and you can only approach it and talk about it in certain ways, and it has to be respected and you can disrespect it in silly ways, make a joke about it and put it in a limerick or you can disrespect it in very serious ways. One of them is, and I ran through all of them in the book that I could think of, one of them is to treat the Holocaust like a historical event like other historical events.

---

1. Alter, Robert. "The Leveling Wind" in *The New Republic*. March 27, 1995. p. 32.

Q: That is to *dis*respect it?

Gass: Yes, because for a great many people the Holocaust is unique and falls outside of history. Otherwise, there might be other Holocausts, there may have been other Holocausts in the past, and this is just a pogrom. This is just a very big one. This is the largest volcanic eruption and now there are lots of volcanoes . . . there'll be more volcanoes and so forth, and people object to the loose use of 'Holocaust' for this that or the other all the time. And there's one whole school of thought that believes that the Holocaust is a non-historical event in the sense that it falls outside history in any usual way. Thus, any attempt to explain it in terms of ordinary causal historical conditioning is to reduce it, to make it something that could have happened in the ordinary run of events. Another way of reducing the Holocaust is to suggest that the Holocaust was not unique to Germany, that it is in principle possible as soon as soon as you say: given such and such circumstances, and such and such conditions and background, Germans were ideal subjects for this, but . . . reproduce them elsewhere and another time. So this is certainly my opinion and one of the reasons that I wrote the book is that I'm not talking about Germany, I'm talking about the United States. So, for the kind of normalization, it's got to be the Germans and it's got to be the Jews and it's got to be an event that is so extraordinary that invertedly this crazy inversion is sacred. And they treat it in all these ways. You have to earn your right to talk about it. For some people like George Steiner, he can't say anything anymore. He went so far as to say he couldn't even write poetry any more but certainly nothing about the Holocaust. So the disrespect that occurs if you put the Holocaust or some event of it or some aspect of it in a limerick—is the bottom. And that's not only characteristic of this guy but it's characteristic of everything I write. I'm disrespectful. I break decorum, I am bad, ill mannered, and in this case it's immoral, because this is something . . . a touch-me-not . . .

Q: *You* don't think it's immoral though, do you . . .

Gass: No. I don't think it's immoral. I think it's essentially moral. It has to be done. But they do.

Q: He's calling your novel obscene because it has a fundamental moral failing. But I don't see, and correct me if I'm wrong, that the novel would have worked with any other event. Could it have been anything other than the Holocaust?

Gass: No. I think I wanted to tackle it . . . in the background, because first of all although as we know as we studied philosophy and looked at history the difficulties every theology is in. We are aware of all of those things and it hasn't done any good; I mean, the problems have not stopped anybody from going on and having these attitudes and beliefs and so forth. The Holocaust is something that really should have raised all those issues in the Jewish community. What is the role of the deity in a world in which this happens? Are we going to do what the people do whose trailer blows up in the trailer park and they escape and say "Thank God!" and they forget that God brought the wind. He's even responsible for trailers, right? (laughs) I mean, so they don't even think about that. It's always: God always gets the good, the good thing. It used to be when something bad happened to the Jews, either they'd broken the covenant, they were being punished, or in fact they would even go so far sometime as to think we haven't broken the covenant, we've kept it, therefore God has broken the covenant. And they took Him to trial. They would have a trial. It's really a contract for some groups. So if this was some terrible thing that happened, God is punishing the Jews for such and such. He's just teaching them. This was a lesson? And what explanation would, in the Jewish community, in any religious community for that matter, are you going to give for this event? And the desperate flight from the confrontation of that and of course, from the suggestions of Hannah Arendt and others that this kind of horror is the piling up of little trivial people doing little stupid, you know, banal things means—

Q: The nickel-and-dime things portrayed in everyday life—

Gass: Yeah right. And, of course, that's what I want them to bring it back to. So I reduce it all, but when I reduce it to fascism of the breakfast table, as I look at it sometime, I'm also trying to ring the changes on the German family: where we learn violence, where we learn these hierarchies, where we learn obedience, and of course it's traditionally been an agent in the explanations of the Holocaust. The German family hierarchy, the kind of obedience and the kind of authoritarianism that that family relationship has built and is characteristically German but is not solely German; so, the fact is that . . . everyone of these people who did these hideous things had a family and a life where they did ordinary things, and it suddenly became an ordinary thing.

But the first problem that confronted people in terms of the Holocaust (not the first, but one of them), wasn't the notion of one person killing another in cold blood and then going off about their ordinary life. Well, we're familiar with that happening—bad enough. I mean, oh that's terrible, but six million?

What about the numbers? I was interested in that. How many does it take to be a real Holocaust. At what point is it something beyond the ordinary in not just numbers of course, but in something like super human. How many home runs does Mac have to hit before he becomes not any longer human but actually a super person or something, you know, but they try to explain the horror of the Holocaust by saying that this is the first case of a sate organizing this whole business and making it in effect legal. Now I didn't try to solve any of these questions in the book. I just raised issues, and what always has astonished me about the whole discussion of the Holocaust is that although there are people trying to come to grips with these issues, they are mostly trying to hide, to get around, to overcome the thing, the problems. No, most of the people who took real great offense to *The Tunnel* were in fact Jews but only some; some of the Jewish reviewers were among my most favorable, but they were the non-believers.

Q: Non believers—?
Gass: They were the Jewish atheists, you know.

Q: Oh, oh.
Gass: Now the rabbis and the people who are really devout aren't going to even see that this book is an attack on anti-Semitism from beginning to end, because it works inside. There's no commitment to the glory of Judaism or anybody or anything else for that matter, and the sense of this is that the Holocaust has taught no one anything. It should have taught these people that they are not living in this sacred religious world. It *has* to be abandoned, that what we have to worry about is the other guy you know, and ourselves, of course. And they don't bring up the resemblances between the Nazi hierarchy and the religious hierarchies. Or of course if you keep the Holocaust a sacred, single, non-historic moment, then you don't have to make comparisons with the Algerians, or notice the difference between the religious confrontations, the racial confrontations, or all of the religious horrors over the centuries. They are not relevant to *this* thing. My view is that they are very relevant. They will talk in one breath about: "well, I had orders and therefore I did such and such" and yet brag about the importance of monotheism. Over and over again, I've referred too, to the superiority of polytheism, ethically, over monotheism, because in polytheism, you don't have objections to other gods. You have all the Gods you want. It is a much better explanational system because the wars and quarrels and the treachery of the gods allow you to make sense of the messes here; whereas, if you have one, you've got insolu-

ble problems. So, as a kind of religious hypothesis, polytheism works much, much better than monotheism. Monotheism is a dictatorship, and the Catholic Church has been a hierarchy and the Jewish Church has been a hierarchy. It's disciplined. It's meanly treated women; it's just awful. And then they go around talking about the Nazis as if. . . . And then also the odd thing they don't confront, which they can avoid, because the Nazis attacked the Communists, by identifying Communism as a Jewish maneuver. So many of the leading intellectuals were Jews, of course, Marx among them. These were the Jews who were not Jews. They were the free thinkers. A similar kind of thing happened, not among Jews, but . . . in this city [St. Louis, Mo.], when, in 1848, when all these revolutions and uprisings took place all over Europe and were put down and a great many of the free thinkers and the socialists were forced to flee Europe, and enormous numbers of Germans came to the United States at that point in time and they were called the "Forty-eighters." You may know all this, but it's fresh to me because we studied all this for our literary history book. They poured into this city and as soon as they came, around 1850 really getting here, they start all these journals attacking all the Catholics, German Catholics who had come earlier, all the Irish, and so forth. And the first thing they did was assault the slavery issue. And they were the abolitionists here and they kept this state of Missouri in the union because they were the abolitionists. But they were attacked on the same grounds, by the Catholics, by the Irish for example. That is, the German Jews, and by other Germans. The socialists were picked on. It is often said that both Communism and Nazism were religious in function and structure and basic nature in lots of ways. So, what always puzzles me is that in religious organizations which are always hierarchical, always dictatorial, always privilege making, always money making, always ruthless, you know, there's no . . . I mean even the Buddhists go out and kill people. There's no history that is without its awfulness in that sense, although the Buddhists get off better than most.

Q: I think when your detractors read this interview, if they do, they're not likely to be pacified, do you think?

Gass: No. Well, I've written a number of other articles, some of which I've published but in relatively obscure journals. One was called "Is There Anything in the World Worth Worship" . . . worth worship at all. And of course no. The argument was nothing is sacred and that includes this.

Q: Some of the reviewers and you yourself have noted that there is a core of nothingness in *The Tunnel;* there is the nothingness that defines the tunnel in Taoist fashion, I suppose; there's the dirt and so forth but the tunnel itself is defined by emptiness. And some reviewers have noted that the novel itself gives us nothing finally. It destroys. It's mean-spirited, we have an utterly despicable character and at the end, there's nothing left to say, there's nothing left to do; not only is nothing sacred, there's a kind of nothingness. Ok. I'm reminded then of Beckett and his claim that his art is an art of failure. One tries, one fails. Why do you keep trying? So I'll fail better next time. Is your art similar?

Gass: Well, I had this argument once with John Gardner and the issue of Beckett was brought up and Gardner was arguing for a more positive conclusion. Certainly I don't think my view is as dark as Beckett's simply because I see a lot of wonderful things along the way. I have a very low opinion of mankind, obviously. And this book is an attack on humanism as much as anything. And one expression was that, of course, now that God is dead, we've fallen into the hands of man, and that is even worse. So what we have to do is look at the historical record, and the historical record is not favorable. And the fact is that this twentieth century was one of the worst, perhaps in history. Those are judgements hard to make, but it certainly was and the strange thing is in the enormous mix of triumphs, of great things, and in the question that Rilke raises in I think "The Eighth Elegy." We did do something great, didn't we? Wasn't there something that we did that justifies our existence or did we do more harm, in general, than good? And I think it very important to be somewhat clear about the evaluation you place on it. The thing is that humanism continues to promulgate the hypocrisy that human beings and their lives are the most important things there are, when in fact we murder and kill and maim and ignore and so forth, people by the tons and the question is maybe they ought to be but they certainly aren't. They're nothing. They're trivial. We throw lives away I think. And everything else. Now there are some wonderful things. And I think the two areas in which wonderful things take place are the arts and the sciences. Scientific endeavor and gaining a knowledge and a creation of things, and Beckett—certainly he's pessimistic. He's not only pessimistic in the work in the sense that there's no relief, there is no relief in his view of things, and also in his person, which is not true, in the sense that he contemplated suicide many times. He was himself, melancholy; every day I damn mankind and I'm not unhappy about it at all. I mean, personally, you know. But the fact is that when I read Beckett, I'm elevated; it's a glorious thing he's done. He's given a beautiful expression to this kind of attitude, this kind of view, this sense of things, and it may not be the true sense but it's a legitimate one, and like any tragedy, you go away feeling a whole lot better because you had the catharsis but nevertheless. And it's the Rilkean thing. Did we do any . . . Chartres was great, he says, wasn't it? Wasn't it? Was it great enough? You know.

Q: The "Archaic Torso of Apollo"—
Gass: Yeah.

Q: The torso's fine enough but then he wrote this poem about it. It's even better, perhaps. So . . . there is progress.
Gass: Well, there's progress; at least good things keep getting made in the midst of the mess. The best answer I think again, in the same line, is Calvino's *Invisible Cities* at the end where he says "We're in hell. What can we do?" *Invisible Cities* is a redoing of the circles of hell with Dante. We live in hell. What can we do? Well, there are two ways of handling it. One is to accept it and go along with it and the other is to resist and to give those who are not of hell, space. Give them help.

Q: And you would see yourself as one of those who is resisting and perhaps Beckett is one who has acquiesced.
Gass: Well, I'm resisting in the sense that I'm yelling about it. I don't know, I think that he was too. His sense of things, however, is I think, further. It is much more Rilkean in the sense that it's metaphysical and therefore inescapable. My anger comes from still thinking it might be (a liberal, a little liberal tendency here) remedied, that it isn't just: "Well, it's the way it is," and sort of resigned to it. It must makes me furious every day, in that sense, this intellectual sense.

Q: The remedy seems to me, at least in what immediately comes to mind in your writings, is not a grand sweeping political solution but has to do with say imagination. I'm thinking in particular of two pieces: "Trapezoidal Mind" and the other one, "The Origin of Extermination in the Imagination" in which you confront very serious social problems. And attribute at least some of our failures to a failing of the imagination and it seems to me that you offer what I would call an aesthetic solution to an ethical problem, a problem of The Other. What about the Turk, the Jew, you know and so forth. In how we react to those, whoever they turn out to be, we may act wrongly; in other words it seems that you are coming down on the side of there being a wrong way to do it.
Gass: Oh, yeah, sure.

Q: And that is a failing of the imagination which to me sounds like an aesthetic solution to what I might say is fundamentally an ethical/social/political problem.

Gass: Well, it might be but imagination is often something that is simply thought of as also an ethical norm. It could be put down as sympathy, empathy or something of the sort, probably, instead of the imagination, but ability to emotionally project yourself into different circumstances, for instance, and the way in which in fact, oh, say someone you love is injured, your own response to the injury which can be—you can even be worse off. I remember my wife cut herself with a hedge trimmer. I almost passed out. I mean, I, it was not that I say something like, "Gee, what if that had happened to me" but it was as if I was feeling it, you know. Everybody has had this. And often, when one is talking about the lack of real sense of how it is for other people and other things or other conditions, you invoke that failure, which is of course one of the things that we make sure doesn't occur when we are training soldiers. You become objects or things or inhuman. But it is often just a lack of the ability sometimes attributed to novelists, to be able to leap into another life and sense how that life is, but if I have any such ability to do that, I've tried to do it for the villain, in that particular book [*The Tunnel*], and try to do it for the villain, who isn't just a cretin, but is a real villain in the Kantian sense, that is he has a lot of other virtues. He doesn't have a good will, but he can be sensitive.

Q: Furber?

Gass: Furber is also like that. They have capacities, they have abilities, and that's another aspect, too. If one studies the Holocaust, though not for very long, one discovers there's no particular station in life, or occupation, or whatever, that enables you to guarantee because you were this sort of, doing this sort of thing, you wouldn't become a Nazi. It cuts across . . . The only escapees were the other fanatics, like Seventh Day Adventists, Jehovah's Witnesses. They had their own fanaticism, they don't need another one. And so they could often be very resistant and brave and morally good in a certain way in which the intellectuals faired terribly, collapsed quickly, didn't have nearly the courage that many ordinary people did. That was also sometimes imagination, being able to project themselves into the situation and understand it so much better, that it was even more crushing. You know, but . . . or if you take Primo Levy, who said once that during the Holocaust, the horrors of the individual person in the camp were so overwhelming that in a certain way you couldn't really think them through, and you only thought them through afterward and that is when you get suicidal. He did apparently throw himself over a railing. But there are arguments about that. So many Holocaust survivors do commit suicide, however. Guilty about still surviving, some think. Or maybe just reliving and digesting it. But I don't think it's necessarily an aesthetic thing. It may be a necessary condition in aesthetic enterprise but I suspect that kind of thing as well as, say, imagining in that sense, at any rate, that ability to imagine must be as much a necessity as being able to think clearly, or perceive or sense adequately the world. So I'd be hesitant to think of it as an aesthetic solution, because I don't think it's that kind of imagination; it's a kind lots of people have who don't necessarily have a certain kind of ability to manipulate a medium in a particular way or they simply show it in different ways, by understanding their colleagues, and so on and so forth, you know.

Q: Let me go off on another tangent. You remarked somewhere, that when you read Rilke for the first time, Rilke, correct me if I misquote you, gave you your thoughts or—

Gass: Well . . .

Q: —gave form to your thoughts.

Gass: Well, it crystallized certain things that I'd been muddling around about in aesthetics, but it certainly did not do so in other ways because I don't share his, his whatever it is, sort of metaphysical views, but in the narrower aesthetic senses, he not only had certain views that I was trying to formulate but he did, there were clear examples and then you could see it being done in lots of ways. And happened also, I had certainly come across and become enamored of Gertrude Stein a lot earlier and Flaubert somewhat, also—they all came together; Rilke just brought them together. They were all in Paris at the same, similar periods: Cézanne, Flaubert, Stein, and Rilke, all within a generation, almost, and they were all doing exactly the same with their mediums and seeing things in a certain fundamental way. He sort of suddenly, coalesced it all for me. Particularly things like what happens to the medium, the very thingness, the idea that to get away from the communication theory of ours, the expressional theories, which when I was beginning, I just knew had been corrupted by the bourgeois, that this was a sort of something they had allowed that was bad. And this sense that Rilke discovers that the poet's aim is to *add* something to reality rather than comment on it or express something, to *be* something; so that, that and lots of other similar kinds of things, the epistemology of a work of art. The transformative issues, all those things I thought were right and didn't solve any fundamental philosophical issues, because even if you now simply say that what the artist does with language is similar, a transformation, ontological transformation the way just perceiving an object is a transformation of the signals into another ontological dimension is still a total mystery. I mean, as far as I'm concerned, for all of the present discussion of the mind/body problem, the division seems to me inescapable still. Consciousness is nowhere. I'd be happy to be a materialist, but it is so clear that consciousness is a function of physical processes and vice versa but consciousness has not been established as a physical thing, to suit me at all, so even if one sees, say, that very problem simply replicated throughout and if the work of art is a process by which the physical world and the experience then becomes experience and that experience is then transformed, not just described, but transformed into language, but the language has also been transformed and then, that has been put out again into the world. So you have an object sitting there which is the result of this big cycle from objects observed by the poet or painter and it's not that the painting is about anything; it is a transformation and a new object in the world.

Q: 'Transformation' sounds weaker than what I would expect you to say, because the nature of a transformation presupposes that you can think both things in sequence or simultaneously, perhaps. The thing that is transformed prior to the transformation and then after it's been transformed. What I would have expected Bill Gass to say is that it doesn't even come to be what it is until it is rendered in language. So, why ever make the comparison in the first place?

Gass: Well, I don't want to absorb the reality of whatever gave rise, including the language itself; let's just say that we have the language of ordinary life and it is used all the time and it has its reality, its ontology, and we have that language, apparently the same words in the poem, and now that poem has *its* reality; *that* transformation is quite different so the words in the poem are not the same at all as the words in ordinary life even though tokens seem the same, sound the same. That I'd certainly hold. Often, this object may have more reality because of its repeatability, its continuous impact, its organization, and so on, than something over here, but I don't want to lose the reality of those things and they have their own, and this is not a substitute and it is not necessarily a superior thing. I mean, I paint a bowl of peaches; I don't want to forget how good the peaches are. The painting is great, and it's greater than the peaches in one sense, but it's important to experience such things as they are, and Rilke is certainly clear about that, such things as the peach or the orange, for example, and grapes in *The Sonnets to Orpheus*— "dance the orange," all those sensuous things, all the appreciations, or standing and looking as I might at the mountain and saying, "Gee that's quite a handsome peak," you know, or something. Or doing, as you suggested of Kant the other day: Kant went out and saw nature and he might say "Ah, sublime!" Now the painting has superiority, I think, in certain obvious ways, but it is also not juicy, I mean, you know, it doesn't nourish, so it doesn't rob the other thing of its dignity and importance and so forth. So, I do certainly argue that, Thucydides' *account* of the Peloponnesian war is far more important historically than the war—

Q: It's what we have.

Gass: That's right. And it's what goes on, and it goes on happening, whereas the war's causal effect is, by this time, lost. It's *really* over, whereas the account is not. And this is part of one of the reasons why we speak of it as being more real. But, to say that doesn't mean that the war wasn't a real thing and wasn't an important series of events, and to rob it of its catastrophe.

Q: No, no, but as an epistemological matter, I'm thinking of Hume, where Hume critiques miracles; he doesn't deny that miracles exist, could exist, have existed, his question is whether you trust the accounts. . . .

Gass: Yeah . . .

Q: . . . of the miracle . . .

Gass: . . . yeah . . .

Q: . . . and his answer is no; so, you've got the account, and the metaphysics of the miracle, let other people ponder that, but no rational person would believe in virgin births, all that sort of thing, because those accounts simply are not trustworthy. Well, now we read—

Gass: *He* doesn't believe them, but everybody else does.

Q: They trust the accounts.

Gass: Sure.

Q: They're not rational on his view.

Gass: I know, but the reality is that that those irrational, non-rational accounts have more effect, and in many measures of reality, not everyone's, are more real. Certainly more real than the event because the accounts are real there whereas the event never happened.

Q: In your view of history, how malleable is history/ Is it utterly malleable?

Gass: I don't think so, no, that's one of the things I argue. Well, I gave this sophistical view to the Nazis of history as malleable only in texts. That view is Fascist; the regime wants to make history into some sort of system that will serve its purposes, which happens over and over again, but, I happen to think that it depends on what you're talking about. If you're talking about historical events as *the things that happened,* then those things happened. They happened once, they happened only in one way and it's a very complex way involving all the consciousness of everybody who was there. But they didn't have two consciousnesses, they had only one and they are complex, too, full of ambiguities, but it was only one *state,* however complicated. And it may very well be that the historian's real job is to try and recover as much as possible of what really happened. The difficulty, of course, is another matter. In the new book, I have a long piece, an essay, on that problem, called "There Was an Old Woman" and it is a version of a piece, I guess, I never get away from these things, of the only philosophical so-called essay I ever wrote, and that was "The Case of the Obliging Stranger." I imagined that there was an old woman who lived in a shoe and that was a shoe on Santa Monica Boulevard near the Brown Derby and she has so many children she *does* know what to do. She eats them. So we go on with the accounts, and I use that as an example to try and show what happens in the interests of why history is such a mess. But I also want to be able to insist that there was something that happened and it really did happen. And it happened in a certain way. And we have to get at it. I also in that piece tried to distinguish between the three fundamental ethical truth-values, and moral values and aesthetic values in terms of their relationship to the data. Mainly, what I wanted to argue was that all the ethical judgements were, in fact, presumably dependent upon an accurate description of the case, whatever it was. And would change, or might, when the facts as presented as an account changed; the moral judgement might change; in that certainly the moral judgement was always directed to and dependent upon the facts. You know she boiled six in a kettle. She did the kettle this way. She did this and that. All of these would be facts, but then the moral reaction to that would depend on those facts, and if they changed, then that judgement would change; and this is not the case with an aesthetic account, because no account of a work of art, no description of a factual character of a work of art, independent of actually experiencing it would give me the *slightest* idea, if I know what I'm doing, of whether its any good aesthetically.

Aesthetically, if somebody describes to me an event that happened like the old woman who eats her children, and I believe this account to be as far as I know correct, then I can have moral revulsion, etc., etc., but if somebody is describing aesthetically, properly, my model and says in it there's. . . . Sure, the wrong-headed people will judge it morally. You shouldn't have said this or this idea is awful or something of the sort. But no aesthetic judgement can be made. You can describe a painting forever factually and no one could get an idea, couldn't make any judgement; you might make a snuff film, describe it, and they'd say, "Oh, my god, how immoral," but if someone said "Oh, but was it gorgeous!" Well, one would be surprised because the idea that somebody who would do a snuff film would have any such capacity would be difficult to take, and one would say it would be difficult to set aside one's moral repugnance to say: "Beautifully done." I think that's within the realm of possibility. That's why I wrote the book, actually. But in any case no description would give you an idea whether a thing was aesthetic or not. See, there's something about moral values which are attached to truth values and to descriptions and something about aesthetic values that is not attached in the same way.

Q: I can imagine Hume saying but who gets to decide on the relations between the accuracy of the factual description so that one can then make the—

Gass: That's another issue. That's a question of whether there is any historical fact at all. What I'm saying at this point is: were there historic facts? or even if (because we do it anyhow) even if the description itself, claiming to be, and you read constantly in the papers, some account of something, and you say, oh, my god! and yet you realize, of course, that were the account to be different, and it might very well be, because you haven't read it all. But from this account, you can say, oh, this is terrible. Now, if they changed the description, you can change your moral judgement and the question is, what about the event itself? That is an epistemological issue, a different one, harder to overcome. I think it can be; there is something that happened. The Holocaust did occur.

Q: Right. Contrary to some—
Gass: Yeah. It really did.

Q: —some insidious revisionists.

Gass: . . . and we do have a lot of information. It's going to be very hard to get at everything and get the right picture, because there's so many interfering morals and emotions, but we can get closer I think, to a balanced picture. But it's a constant revision, and it *is* dialectical, in the sense that new accounts come along and challenge the old, and often the old account has to give way to a certain degree, at any rate, and that continues all the time; but it doesn't mean that because we are going to be wrong about some things, we're wrong about everything. I don't think that's true at all.

Q: Point taken. Let me ask you something. Do we still have time?
Gass: Sure.

Q: Okay, back to your comments about reading Rilke and your reaction to Rilke. What I was going to ask is whether the process, and I think the answer is going to be no, was similar to what happens to Emma when she enters her sentence and keeps hearing fragments of sentences. Is that process for you in any way analogous to your reaction to Rilke?

Gass: Her entering is the wrong way.

Q: It's the wrong way?

Gass: She's trying to get salvation. She's trying to escape her existence, I think. She doesn't really understand a poem, she can't read them correctly, but she has a sense of the better thing there, of some values that aren't being achieved in the world that she knows. In part she's herself achieving some of them, because she's aware that she is observing and part of that is Rilkean in fact, in the book, over and over again, the clairvoyant and other elements of the book, the Rilkean observer of the world is invoked in a certain sense. Almost immediately it's twisted; she's trapped, I mean, and again, there's no way out. This is an inadequate . . . well, there ain't no salvation.

Q: But isn't she better off?
Gass: Well, sure, sure.

Q: So in that sense, maybe it's construable as an escape. But one could say she's achieving Being whereas before . . .
Gass: Yeah, yeah.

Q: . . . she had no being at all.
Gass: Yeah.

Q: . . . so it is a kind of ontological transformation, if I could push that a little . . .

Gass: Sure.

Q: . . . and through language.

Gass: Through language, yeah. I wouldn't let her *be*. . . . That sort of thing happens to almost every adolescent; they go through it for a period, often those seek refuge in books from the world. Certainly I did; but I'm hard on my characters and wouldn't give her very much real grasp; it's a glimpse; she's getting glimpses, as she is from observing things around her, getting glimpses of something better, something more important . . .

Q: You let her be righteously indignant about her father finally.

Gass: Oh, yeah . . .

Q: I thought, Okay, that's good, this is a good thing.

Gass: She hits him. He *dies*.

Q: When I got to the end . . . didn't expect that to happen. I thought the ending too, for those who would constantly claim that Gass is bleak, Gass is bleak, well, not that that's happy but one can feel a sort of, not exactly warm and fuzzy, but that something correct has been done.

Gass: Oh yeah.

Q: vengeance, righteous vengeance . . .

Gass: Oh yeah. There's a feminist strain in the piece of course. Yeah. It is in fact something of the relationship of male and female in that regard. . . .

Q: Or at the risk of stating the obvious, one can see the whole thing as a critique of pornography in that what you're doing is destroying the fundamentally pornographic way in which men interact with women.

Gass: Yeah sure . . . He deserved it because he cut the tree down. (laughter)

Q: Okay, a semi-personal question. What happens to *you* when you write? You have said that writing for you is sometimes fitful, always fitful. There's anger involved, . . .

Gass: Oh, well . . .

Q: You're miserable when you're not writing and that the writing itself is . . .

Gass: Yeah, it's hard because it . . . because it's a constant lack of success, I mean, and it isn't getting any better even though you may be more facile about things now than you were when starting out. It's a constant perception of inadequacy and that's sort of low-grade misery, but while I'm writing, it's a kind of work. I know things are going well when I'm really into it. I'm not distracted, I forget the time, etc. You know, you're really, in a sense, concentrating. It doesn't mean it's going to be good but it means that you are producing and *into the piece,* and that's always crucial for me. I really have to get *into it* somehow.

Q: Into it in the sense that in which the text that you're writing becomes a container for your own consciousness?

Gass: No, the text starts to take over and makes its own demands, until I get that going, and that's true of even shorter pieces, or essays. It doesn't matter what I'm doing in a way, until the thing gets its own character, and then I have to get into *it.* The trouble with, say, *The Tunnel,* was, among many things and prolonged it, was, that I had a long period of time in which I could not figure out what I was doing really, and so there were lots of breaks, and so I was coming back to it, coming back to it presumably as a different person to some degree, because ten years might pass. I'm working on it all the time, a little bit, and you want to be the same writer who started it. That isn't possible. The advantage I had was that this was in the first person, in the narrator, and I had to get into the narrator's head, and he was strong enough; I don't mean that in a good sense, but a strong enough character, in the defining properties so that it was possible for me to get back into him in order to continue the book. Once I had created his consciousness, his type, then when I had a lay-off, whether it was weeks or months or so, I could still eventually get back into his frame and then go on with the book. In other pieces, the piece itself may not be a consciousness but it's a frame of mind, a mode, a pattern. I'm writing a piece now where the language is much much simpler. I'm not allowed lyric rifts and junk, because the book has just developed that way. It's got a different tone, and each piece has that or I try to get that for it, and so it has its rhythms, its atmosphere, and that's what I need and that's what I have to pay attention to; and it's difficult. That means you have to leave aside whatever frames or frame of mind you might have come to the machine with, find *it* and get *it* back, whatever is there.

Q: I'm puzzled a little bit. Your concept of character, as I understand it, it is not as if a character is sort of a surrogate human being or a surrogate consciousness but is rather like a anchor in the language around which lots of sentences revolve.

Gass: It's a noun qualified by the rest of the text; it's Hegelian.

Q: So when you're getting into the character, so to speak, is it that you're getting into his, getting into the language that would flow—

Gass: Well, that would work with this guy, because he's the whole book. Everything in it qualifies him. If it's not that, if I'm working with another piece, then it isn't that I'm getting into a character the way I would get into Emma or something, in that traditional sense. It's getting into the text in general and its construction.

Q: Okay.

Gass: Yeah. It happens in *The Tunnel* to be a consciousness of a person that is the whole damn thing in a way, but in other cases in fact it's a consciousness overriding. One critic objected to it. I override the characters in several pieces in *The Cartesian Sonata.* That is, just as you might have an omniscient narrator describing things in the world, I am describing the interior of somebody's mind but with *my* vocabulary, not theirs. *My* observations, not necessarily theirs, and it's a device, and it's one of the methods but one reviewer particularly objected to, the fact that I overrode. He must just object; he had something else he wanted to object to and I couldn't get to it, I think, because there are so many cases of this in literature that this is just one technique, but anyway. Getting back into it is really a matter of getting that sense of relevance so that you've gotten the connectives and you're sensitive to them and everything is connecting, but you're also in the music and the mood and the pace of it. It's one reason I like novellas because it's easier to stay inside for all the piece until it's done. It's harder for a novel; it's really hard. It's the hardest thing about writing a novel, I think. This sustained creating that so-called author and being the author who's writing my book for years.

Q: For decades.

Gass: Yeah, in my case, it is. And in some others, of course.

Q: What can we expect next?

Gass: Well, the next book is just gone to press, or gone to the publisher. That is another collection of essays, but I held back a bunch of them to formulate a book that's basically social-political, takes up moral issues and things of that sort. It's much more also directed toward a lot of the cultural issues of the day, so it's more current in that sense, than my other things, and I'm almost finished with another book of novellas, I thought; I got two of them done I was working on and one's called *In Camera* that just came out in *Conjunctions* and then the other one is called *Charity* then and the third one is *Middle C* and it's in the middle. If one is about photography, this one's about music. But the piece threatens to be a novel.

Q: Threatens to be . . .

Gass: I think it's gotten away from what I have thought it would be. And certainly it's about someone who has musical abilities and so forth but it's oddly the ethical issue, an ethical issue of how to avoid responsibility.

Index